Foucault – The Key Ideas

Teach
Yourself®

Foucault –
The Key Ideas
Paul Oliver

For UK order enquiries: please contact Bookpoint Ltd,
130 Milton Park, Abingdon, Oxon OX14 4SB.
Telephone: +44 (0) 1235 827720. Fax: +44 (0) 1235 400454.
Lines are open 09.00–17.00, Monday to Saturday, with a 24-hour
message answering service. Details about our titles and how to
order are available at www.teachyourself.com

For USA order enquiries: please contact McGraw-Hill Customer
Services, PO Box 545, Blacklick, OH 43004-0545, USA.
Telephone: 1-800-722-4726. Fax: 1-614-755-5645.

For Canada order enquiries: please contact McGraw-Hill Ryerson
Ltd, 300 Water St, Whitby, Ontario L1N 9B6, Canada.
Telephone: 905 430 5000. Fax: 905 430 5020.

Long renowned as the authoritative source for self-guided
learning – with more than 50 million copies sold worldwide –
the *Teach Yourself* series includes over 500 titles in the fields of
languages, crafts, hobbies, business, computing and education.

British Library Cataloguing in Publication Data: a catalogue record
for this title is available from the British Library.

Library of Congress Catalog Card Number: on file.

First published in UK 2010 by Hodder Education, part of Hachette
UK, 338 Euston Road, London NW1 3BH.

First published in US 2010 by The McGraw-Hill Companies, Inc.

This edition published 2010.

The **Teach Yourself** name is a registered trade mark of Hodder
Headline.

Typeset by MPS Limited, A Macmillan Company.

Printed and bound in Great Britain by Clays Ltd, Elcograf S.p.A.

The publisher has used its best endeavours to ensure that the URLs
for external websites referred to in this book are correct and active
at the time of going to press. However, the publisher and the
author have no responsibility for the websites and can make no
guarantee that a site will remain live or that the content will remain
relevant, decent or appropriate.

Hachette UK's policy is to use papers that are natural, renewable
and recyclable products and made from wood grown in sustainable
forests. The logging and manufacturing processes are expected to
conform to the environmental regulations of the country of origin.

Impression number   10 9 8 7 6
Year   2019

Contents

Meet the author

Welcome to *Foucault – The Key Ideas*!

I currently teach at the University of Huddersfield, England. I am the course leader for a Master's programme in Religion and Education, as well as the course leader for the Doctor of Education programme. I teach comparative religion and also social science research methods, in addition to supervising doctoral research students in related areas. I have a Master of Philosophy degree for research in the Sikh religion, and my Doctor of Philosophy degree was for a study of the social context of Hinduism.

In terms of writing, I have been the sole author of eight books and have been editor or joint editor of a further five books. The main areas to which I contribute books are philosophy, comparative religion and research methodology. I am a former editor of the *Journal of Vocational Education and Training*. I have also written eleven chapters in edited books, and my own books have been translated into seven languages.

Paul Oliver, 2010

Only got a minute?

Michel Foucault was one of the leading thinkers of the twentieth century and continues to be hugely influential in the twenty-first.

Born in Poitiers, France, in 1926, he grew up during a troubled time in French history and as a teenager experienced war and occupation by the Nazis. The post-war period was also a time of great intellectual ferment, with the development of the existentialist ideas of Jean-Paul Sartre, a figure with whom Foucault is often compared and contrasted.

By the 1960s he had established a prestigious career as an academic within the French university system and in 1968 became involved with the radical student activism centred on the Parisian universities. Despite his radical reputation, however, Foucault found wide acclaim for a series of groundbreaking, challenging books such as *Madness and Civilization* (1961) – a study of the changing attitudes to the insane – and *Discipline and Punish* (1975) – a study of the institution of the prison.

At the heart of Foucault's work was a passionate empathy for the dispossessed and a desire to trace the subtle networks of power characteristic of contemporary society. Foucault died in Paris in 1984 from an AIDS-related illness.

5 Only got five minutes?

Michel Foucault (1926–84) has been one of the key thinkers of the post-war world. For many people he replaced Jean-Paul Sartre as arguably the leading intellectual figure in Europe, and perhaps the world.

Rather ironically, one of Foucault's criticisms of Sartre was that the latter represented the ideal of the universal intellectual, someone who attempted to construct a model of society that he believed, implicitly or explicitly, others should follow. Foucault always said that he preferred neither to follow a particular academic school of thought, nor to establish one himself. Yet, Foucault's many followers have tended to defy his wishes. They have articulated his views of society, founded academic journals devoted to research within the perspectives he established, and cited him in countless academic papers. Above all, Foucault's memory seems to be maintained by the many, many contemporary students of the humanities, education and the social sciences who quote his works and use examples from his writing.

Foucault was a distinctive figure, partly because of his striking, almost monk-like appearance, but also because he often placed himself in the limelight, arguing for moral and political causes, many of which were either unpopular, or even unheard of, before Foucault took them up. Although Sartre and Foucault were often cast by people in opposition to each other, and although it was true that they sometimes critiqued each other's work, they were often to be found shoulder to shoulder fighting the same cause. The best example of this was during the 1968 student unrest in Paris.

Foucault was unconventional in many different ways: in his personal life, in his style of writing and research, in the subject matter he chose to write about, and sometimes in the intellectual positions he chose to adopt. He was part of a post-war, postmodern French intellectual tradition that included academics such as Derrida, Lyotard, Bourdieu, Deleuze and Lacan who transformed the social sciences and humanities. Foucault changed the way in which we think about power, and the way in which it functions in society. He gave us a new way of conceiving of historical development and of the times of transition in history. He turned his attention to issues as different as sexuality, prison reform, the nature of punishment, the Islamic revolution in Iran, and the way in which madness has been conceptualized and treated throughout history. He identified and examined, in rigorous detail, unusual historical case studies that had been only rarely investigated before, in order to provide material with which to illustrate his theories.

Foucault anticipated many of the features of contemporary society, which we have come to, if not accept, at least recognize as an almost inevitable component of modern life. He pointed to the growth of organizations and institutions in the postmodern age, and the depersonalizing nature of much of their activities. The latter included, in particular, the focus upon observation of individuals, so that each of us is never certain whether or not we are being watched by the authorities. He analysed the relationship between the power exercised by institutions and the type of discourse that was accepted within those organizations. Moreover, he related that discourse to the kinds of knowledge that become accepted as valid within such institutions.

Michel Foucault is arguably one of the most significant intellects of the twentieth century, in the areas of the humanities and the social sciences. He simply gave us a different way of looking at the world.

1

Themes of a life

In this chapter you will learn about:
* *the key events in the life of Michel Foucault*
* *the main historical and political events that provided a backdrop to his life*
* *an overview of his academic development and of his main intellectual ideas.*

Early life and influences

Paul-Michel Foucault was born on 15 October 1926 in Poitiers, France. Poitiers is the capital of the Poitou-Charentes region, in western central France, and is home to the country's second oldest university, whose former students have included such luminaries as the writer François Rabelais (c. 1494–1553) and the philosopher René Descartes (1596–1650). Foucault thus grew up in a historic town with important academic and cultural links, and would have been very used to university life, even before he himself became a student.

Another influence on the development of Foucault must have been the events of World War II. After the Nazi invasion of France in 1940, Poitiers became part of Vichy France (1940–44), the unoccupied southern zone of the country that was essentially a puppet state of the German Third Reich. Later in the war the city was occupied and came under direct Nazi rule. The war was a period of anxiety and uncertainty for the people of Poitiers and we can only assume that the experience had a profound effect on the developing world view of the teenage Foucault.

Foucault's father, Paul, was a successful surgeon and the family was consequently financially secure, enjoying such luxuries as household servants. The father appears to have exerted strict control over the family. He evidently became unhappy with the development of his eldest son, and he sent him for a very formal education at the local Roman Catholic high school. The young Michel was expected to follow a career in medicine. However, it soon became apparent that the boy had a strong independent streak and would forge his own career path.

Insight

For most of his life, Foucault was a person who rejected authority and the accepted norms. His early refusal to follow a career in medicine is perhaps an indication of this tendency.

Somehow Foucault managed to persuade his parents to allow him to pursue an academic career and to try to obtain a place at the Ecole normale supérieure in Paris. This was one of the most celebrated institutions of the *grandes écoles* system of France. Traditionally these specialist higher education institutions provided courses of training and education for a select few who would ultimately occupy leading positions in the professions. The Ecole normale supérieure was the leading institution for obtaining a post in a French university to teach Humanities. Entry was selective, and young people from across France competed for places. In order to maximize their chances of entry, candidates often studied at the so-called *khâgne* classes at a Paris *lycée* (secondary school). These involved a year of intense study, leading up to the entry examination.

To this end, in 1945 Foucault left home and travelled to Paris to enrol at the Lycée Henri-IV. This is one of the premier *lycées* of France, situated on the rue Clovis, in the 5th arrondissement of Paris. The *khâgne* courses were extremely demanding, requiring a great deal of private study and reading. Foucault impressed his tutors and at the end of the academic year was successful in gaining entry to the Ecole normale on the rue d'Ulm. He was now a *normalien*, and his real development towards becoming an intellectual began.

University life in Paris

The course at the Ecole normale lasted four years. At the end of the course the students sat the examinations for the *agrégation*, the qualification that allowed the holder to teach in the French higher education system. Foucault specialized in Philosophy and familiarized himself with the leading French and German philosophers. While he was acknowledged by fellow students and tutors alike to be highly intelligent, he was also considered to have a somewhat unusual, even difficult, personality.

While at university Foucault showed signs of being unhappy and disturbed. Of course, this isn't particularly unusual for students, who are trying very hard to find their true persona and to identify a route through life which they find interesting and appealing. Young people at this age are often caught between the advice and indeed demands of parents, and their own developing interests. The two are often in conflict. This can be all the harder for university students since they are trying to develop their own world view within an environment that includes highly intelligent, accomplished and articulate peers.

In 1948, two years after starting at the Ecole normale, Foucault's anxieties culminated in a suicide attempt. There is no reliable evidence for his immediate motivation in attempting to take his own life, other than his general feeling of unhappiness. In addition, there is no way of knowing whether he was serious about the attempt, or whether it was intended as a kind of public statement of his unhappiness. At any rate, it must have been very disturbing for his parents, who had no doubt great hopes of their son having a successful career as a university lecturer. His father arranged for

Michel to have a psychiatric assessment and gradually the event seems to have been forgotten. However, it was a precursor of a lifelong interest, one might say obsession, of Foucault's with suicide and death. He appears to have held the belief in later life that the contemplation, and indeed the act of suicide, was an acceptable activity. At the end of his four-year course, he initially failed the *agrégation*, but passed it a year later in 1951. This initial failure might be taken as a further indication of maladjustment to his current life.

Another trend in his student years that was to presage a major theme of his private life in later years was his developing homosexuality. There had been indications of this earlier in his life, but during his years at the Ecole normale his attraction to men became pronounced and he began to take part in the gay subculture of Paris. It should be remembered, however, that in the early 1950s there was not an overt gay scene of the kind that would evolve in the capital a few decades later. Even though Paris had a justified reputation as a liberal city, gay liaisons and activities were normally conducted surreptitiously. Foucault, however, made no particular attempt to hide his predilections from fellow students at the Ecole normale. Students then, as now, were generally eager for new experiences, and tolerant of those who sought them. Foucault may have been considered a little different, but probably no more, in his own way, than many other students.

Insight

Foucault's evolving homosexuality may have been the cause of developing psychological tensions. It is unclear whether his parents were aware of his sexuality but, if so, then it may have been the cause of further tension between Foucault and his father.

A noteworthy influence during his period at the Ecole normale was that of Louis Althusser (1918–90), the Marxist philosopher and Communist Party activist. He had started work as a philosophy tutor at the Ecole normale about halfway through Foucault's course and Foucault attended his lectures. Althusser seems to have had a considerable influence upon his students, and one might assume that this also applied to Foucault. It seems plausible that Althusser's lectures were at least one of the factors that resulted in Foucault's joining the Communist Party, which he did after graduation in 1951.

As someone who was developing a world view that tended to reject the significance for society of individual, subjective action, it seems reasonable that Foucault should have been influenced by the **structuralist** theories of Karl Marx (1818–83). Although Marx was a wide-ranging thinker, Foucault tended to be influenced by the strand of thought that individual existence was predominantly shaped by the large-scale structures and institutions of society. Society influenced the individual, rather than the other way round. However, as we shall note throughout this book, a sweeping generalization such as this ignores the enormous diversity of Foucault's thinking. It is exceedingly difficult to put Foucault into a neat intellectual box and say that he belongs to a specific school of thought. Indeed, on a number of occasions, Foucault himself asserted that very point, stressing, for example, that he never adopted one particular theoretical perspective in his research or a particular methodology of collecting and analysing data. He appears to have selected whichever methodology appeared to be appropriate for the problem he had set himself; and in some instances, he developed what he argued were *new* methodologies.

Insight

At various times commentators upon Foucault have tried to attach labels to his writing. However, during his lifetime Foucault tended to reject such labels. It can therefore be difficult to position his work in relation to, for example, that of his contemporaries.

Early career development

After graduation Foucault obtained a post as a tutor at the Ecole normale, probably partly through the support of Althusser and other professors. This involved providing some individual support to students. Two years after graduating, and while still retaining the tutorship at the Ecole normale, he was successful in obtaining a lectureship in Psychology at the University of Lille. During this period at Lille he published his first book, *Maladie mentale et psychologie* ('Psychology and Mental Illness'; published 1954). Foucault had now been studying hard and continuously for a long time, and, like many people in that position, felt that he needed a break from the academic world. Indeed he may even have felt that he was not suited to the life of a university lecturer. He managed to obtain a post as cultural attaché at the University of Uppsala in Sweden, a role that did not involve the kind of teaching responsibilities to which he had been accustomed. He probably gained this post partly through the influence of Georges Dumezil (1898–1986), who was then a professor at the Collège de France, but who had taught at Uppsala during the early 1930s. He was nearly 30 years older than Foucault, but throughout the latter's life would intervene on many occasions to support his academic development. He was destined to outlive his young protégé.

After four years at Uppsala, Foucault moved again, this time to Poland. The French Cultural Centre in Warsaw had been reopened and Foucault was appointed the director. However, it seems that aspects of his private life caused concern there, and he began to consider returning to his homeland. It was suggested to him that he might consider a lecturing vacancy in the Philosophy Department at the University of Clermont-Ferrand. The head of the department was somewhat familiar with Foucault's work, and ultimately he was successful in obtaining the job. Thus, by the beginning of the 1960s, Foucault was successfully reinstalled in France and back within the academic world.

He now also began work on completing his doctoral theses. At this time in France, it was necessary to produce two theses in order to achieve a doctorate. His shorter thesis was on the work of the German philosopher Immanuel Kant (1724–1804), and was examined by Jean Hippolyte, Foucault's former teacher at the Lycée Henri-IV. The major thesis, which was an enormous work of almost one thousand pages, was entitled *Folie et déraison: histoire de la folie à l'âge classique.* This would be translated into English and published in 1982 as *Madness and Civilization: A History of Insanity in the Age of Reason.* The committee of academics who conducted the viva voce examination for the major thesis expressed some surprise at the unconventional academic style in which it was written, while at the same time acknowledging its detailed, scholarly approach.

The basic argument of *Madness and Civilization* was contrary to received wisdom about the insane. The contemporary assumption, derived from a scientific-psychological model of mental illness, was that it could be defined and described in terms of a cognitive malfunction. Foucault, however, argued that people were often defined as insane simply because they behaved in ways that were different from the majority or that contravened the norms of polite society. In other words, madness was a question of social and cultural definition. This argument in itself was somewhat disconcerting for the scientifically oriented members of Foucault's doctoral assessment panel. He also argued that during the medieval period there had been a tendency to treat those who were mentally disturbed as simply different from the norm while still according them a place in everyday society. However, with the Enlightenment, the eighteenth-century 'age of science and rationality', there develops a philosophy of excluding the insane from normal society and placing them under surveillance in separate institutions. They are punished and given what is regarded as remedial treatment. Attempts are made to coerce them back into normal patterns of behaviour. Foucault did not paint a complimentary picture of contemporary society, and this was not lost on the doctoral examiners. Nevertheless, there was an appreciation that they were faced with an impressive piece of work, and an original thinker.

Insight

The idea that society defines people in a particular way is an increasingly popular one. For example, we might argue that disabled people are only 'disabled' if they define themselves as such, or if society defines them in that way.

While at Clermont-Ferrand, Foucault met a philosophy lecturer named Daniel Defert (1937–), who would remain his long-term partner. However, in 1966 Defert had to commence his military service and was scheduled to serve this in Tunisia. Foucault wanted to remain with Defert and managed to obtain a lecturing position at the University of Tunis. He and Defert lived in a small seaside town named Sidi Bou Said, about 15 miles from Tunis itself. This was famous as an artists' colony: among others, Paul Klee had painted there. The town is popular with tourists, being famous for its striking houses with their dazzling whitewashed walls and cobalt-blue shutters.

It was during 1966 that Foucault published his next book, *Les Mots et les choses: une archéologie des sciences humains,* which was later published in English translation as *The Order of Things: An archaeology of the human sciences*. While Foucault ranged far and wide in this work, at its heart, I would argue, is the concept of the **episteme**. Each period in history, Foucault argued, was characterized by an interweaving network of assumptions about the world that conditioned the beliefs and propositions that were accepted as true. Some ideas would not be seriously considered by society because they fell outside the distinctive set of assumptions, or ways of thinking, that were a feature of that epoch. Sometimes these ways of thinking would be overt and fully in the public consciousness, and sometimes they would be less overt, perhaps even part of the collective subconscious. At any rate, they functioned to determine what society considered to be scientific or rational. The sum total of this complex relationship of ideas that determined the nature of public thought was termed the 'episteme'. Gradually, and through a varied range of historical, political, economic and other factors, the nature of the context and limitations of public consciousness would evolve, and one episteme would gradually be transformed into another. This idea would be a central element in Foucault's thought in subsequent publications.

Just as Foucault was thinking intellectually about changes in the parameters of human thought, dramatic changes were also afoot in the political life of France. In early 1968 the Vietnam War (1959–75) was at its height. Around the world there were growing objections to the morality and conduct of the war. On 16 March an American patrol in Vietnam fired on a small village named My Lai and killed many of the inhabitants. The massacre was to further intensify the moral outrage against the war, but, even before the full details emerged, on 17 March there was a large anti-war demonstration in London's Grosvenor Square. In April students protesting against the war occupied Columbia University in New York City.

Besides the Vietnam War, there were, however, other sources of discontent among young people. On 19 March, students at Howard University in Washington, DC, protested against the alleged biased nature of the university teaching, in not taking sufficient account of Afro-American culture. Three days later a student activist named Daniel Coln-Bendit, along with other students, occupied the University of Nanterre in Paris, as a protest against the actions of what they saw as a conservative educational establishment. This was to be the precursor of events that two months later would almost cause the collapse of the French government. For Foucault in Sidi Bou Said, however, the world continued in a relatively tranquil sequence of teaching, research and writing.

Insight

The late 1960s was a period of enormous social change, in all aspects of life. In the key areas of race and gender, especially, there was a gathering movement calling for change. Some of the activists' demands would later become enshrined in legislation that would begin to transform society in these areas.

During April complaints and protests at Nanterre continued, culminating in the closure of the university. Protests broke out at the Sorbonne in Paris, and that too was closed. Street protests were met with hardline policing, and there were arrests and injuries. Events culminated on the evening of 10 May, with the erection of barricades in the Latin Quarter of Paris, and full-scale violent conflict between students and police. Unions and workers across France gradually became involved in the disputes and a general strike was called for 13 May. A large part of the economic life and social infrastructure of

France came to a halt. President de Gaulle called an election for 23 June. Foucault was able to keep in fairly close contact with what was happening in France and, at the end of May, he returned to Paris.

Growing fame

In taking action, students were undoubtedly in part motivated by a dislike of the educational establishment and wanted reform in the universities and *lycées*; the workers, by contrast, were no doubt more concerned by their demands for improved wages and working conditions. Nonetheless, in the June national elections de Gaulle was returned to power and reaffirmed as president. However, the unrest made the government realize that reforms were essential. A new university campus was planned for Vincennes near Paris and during the summer Foucault was invited to become the new head of the Philosophy Department. The idea of Vincennes was that it would be a new type of university, more democratic, and built around the ideas supported by the student protestors. Foucault accepted the post and started putting into place his ideas for the new department.

The university was originally known as the Experimental University Centre of Vincennes, but after the reorganization of Paris universities would eventually become the Paris VIII University. The creation of the institution was supported by Edgar Faure (1908–88), the Minister for National Education. It would eventually provide courses in areas of the social sciences and humanities not previously available in Paris universities. Foucault started to appoint lecturers in his new department, some of whom had been involved in the various radical movements of May 1968. The university admitted its first students in January 1969.

However, the idea of direct student action was still not over in France. The new university had only been open for several days, when a group of staff, including Foucault, as well as students, occupied some of the buildings as a protest against recent police action at the Sorbonne. The police arrived and there was a confrontation – the activists barricaded parts of the building and missiles were thrown at the police. Foucault was fully involved in the action, and from this event arose his reputation as a focus for left-wing protest against conservative values in France.

The same year as his involvement in this new university saw the publication of his next major work, *L'Archéologie du savoir*, which was published in an English edition in 1972, as *The Archaeology of Knowledge*. This book was fundamentally on social science and historical methodology, and set out to explore two fundamental issues involving epistemes. Foucault used the term **archaeology** to refer to the exploration of the manner in which one episteme could gradually replace another, and the term **genealogy** to refer to an examination of the causal factors that might contribute to the way in which ideas change and evolve. Foucault would employ this conceptual framework in some of his future research.

In the meantime Foucault was beginning to be transformed into a more radical and politically engaged figure. His partner, Daniel Defert, had also obtained a post as Professor of Sociology at Vincennes, and the two of them had been jointly involved in the disturbances of early 1969. Defert, and to some extent Foucault, had also become associated with the Gauche prolétarienne, an extreme left-wing faction. Partly as a result of this involvement, in 1970 Foucault established the Groupe d'information sur les prisons (GIP), whose prime purpose was to publicize the sometimes less than pleasant conditions within the French prison system. The organization had a relatively rapid success and in 1970, as a result of its lobbying, journalists were granted permission to enter some prisons to report on conditions.

Insight

Foucault's work with the GIP is an example of how Foucault was able to influence the policy of the French authorities, and perhaps also of the capacity of intellectual ideas to have an impact upon practical situations. Indeed, there is a history in France of respect for philosophers and for the importance of the 'intellectual'.

Life as a leading academic

In 1970 Foucault also won significant recognition from the French academic establishment. He was appointed to a professorship at the Collège de France. This institution, located close to the Sorbonne, was founded by François I in 1530 and over the centuries had become primarily a research institution. There are only about fifty professors at the Collège, and they are appointed by a vote of the existing members. The Collège has an interesting open-access system: although it does not award qualifications, the lecture programme that it provides is open to members of the public and there is no charge for admission. Professors are normally selected from those who are at the forefront of research in their particular subject and their teaching commitments are not exacting. Foucault was expected to give an annual series of lectures, while at the same time continuing with his research. His position at the Collège de France enabled him to continue with his research and writing, while at the same time having considerable status within the French intellectual establishment.

Foucault's interest in the contemporary French prison system was mirrored by an academic interest in the forms of punishment that had evolved over the centuries within the judicial system. In 1975 he published a major work, *Surveiller et punir: naissance de la prison*, which was published two years later in English translation as *Discipline and Punish: The birth of the prison*. In this book Foucault contrasts the extreme physical cruelty of the punishment meted out in the eighteenth century with the long-term incarceration typical of punishment in the twentieth century. In both instances, however, Foucault wanted to analyse the nature of a society that could exercise such extensive control over individuals. Moreover, while the nature of the modern prison was the focus of his analysis, he was also very interested in the way that some organizational features of prisons were employed, in one form or another, within other institutions of society.

One of Foucault's major interests was in the use of observation, which, he argued, reflected the power and authority structures within society. Just as prisoners are closely observed all the time, as a strategy for controlling them, similar techniques could be used in urban areas, which has to in urban areas, which has to a large extent replaced the presence of police officers on the streets. The continual observation of citizens reduces the need to have the forces of law and order continually present. They can be called upon when observations suggest they are required.

Insight

One of the strengths of the observational system is that the *capacity* to observe is usually sufficient in itself. In other words, if citizens merely think they might be observed, then this is often sufficient motivation to transform or constrain their behaviour.

Another of Foucault's ideas was that prisoners are frequently judged in terms of the extent to which they comply with expected behaviour patterns. This is notably so when, for example, they apply for parole. Their behaviour is compared with an 'ideal type' of prison behaviour in order to decide whether they are suitable for remission of their sentence. Once again, Foucault argued, such a comparison of human behaviour with accepted societal norms is a significant feature of our wider contemporary society, including for example, when certain types of behaviour are defined as deviant.

The third feature of prisons that interested Foucault was that of the examination. Prisoners wishing for a curtailment of their sentence must submit to an examination of their personality and behaviour patterns. Similarly, the idea of the examination has permeated most aspects of society, whether this is the driving test, academic examinations, or professional examinations. In most instances, detailed observation is combined with a careful comparison with expected norms.

Insight

In pointing out the importance of examinations and testing in contemporary society, Foucault was implicitly indicating the failings of such a system. A preoccupation with testing often attaches an exaggerated importance to the testing process itself, rather than the skill or knowledge being tested.

In 1975 Foucault received an invitation to become a visiting professor at the University of California, Berkeley. Although he had taught briefly in New York before, he was less familiar with the West Coast. He was not widely known in the United States, except among a small, enthusiastic coterie of academics. Foucault was excited by California, and its liberal atmosphere, which he found contrasted strongly with the more conservative values of his native France. He experimented with hallucinogenic drugs, and was absorbed by, and participated in, the gay social life of San Francisco. His personal experiences here contributed to his academic work, for he was in the process of researching and writing *Histoire de la sexualité: Vol. 1, La Volonté de savoir*. This was published the following year in 1976, and appeared in English two years later as the first volume of *The History of Sexuality*.

In this study Foucault surveyed the changing and evolving attitudes to sexuality over the centuries. He argued that at different periods in history, society held very different attitudes to sex. In the pre-Christian world, for example, sexuality, he argued, was much more within the realm of the individual person. It was seen as a source of pleasure, as much as, or perhaps more than, a means of continuing the species. The State tended not to involve itself in the habits and practices of individuals. The rise of Christian Europe, however, saw the development of a different moral position. Abstinence from sexual activity was now perceived as an example of Christian piety and was encouraged. Vows of abstinence among monastic communities and the clergy were considered a serious matter, and infringements were often a matter for harsh punishment. The church established norms for what was considered acceptable behaviour. The sexual act was perceived primarily as a reproductive act, to be conducted as an element of the Christian life. Sex, in the eyes of the church, was not for personal gratification.

With the gradual demise of a theocratic control of society, Foucault noted the increasing involvement of the State and legislature in the regulation of sexuality. What was and was not acceptable in society was increasingly defined by statute. Legislation came to define many aspects of sexual activity. The legislature defined where it might take place, with whom and within what age limits. Moreover, the judicial system could pass judgement on activities undertaken in a private home, and proclaim some acceptable, and others not so. Some private activities might be seen as contravening public norms. Foucault saw these developments as another example of the power of the State to define the limits of human action.

Foucault, meanwhile, had maintained a general interest in the role of the intellectual as a political commentator, and indeed activist. In 1978 events broke out in Iran that would have considerable repercussions for world politics. In January 1978 there were the first public protests against the American-supported regime of Shah Mohammad Pahlavi. The protesters were in favour of the Shi'a Islamic movement led by Ayatollah Khomeini. There were further protests during 1978 and the Shah appealed to President Carter for American aid. The political opposition was against what they saw as the repressiveness of the Shah's regime and the self-serving nature of his government. The activists also militated against the Western economic involvement in Iran. On Friday, 8 September, there was a large protest in Teheran, followed by police repression, and a number of protesters were killed. Foucault had been following events in Iran and was commissioned by an Italian newspaper to visit the country and write a series of articles on the situation. Foucault arrived in Teheran just after what became known as 'Black Friday'.

From the beginning, Foucault was very enthusiastic about the developing revolution in Iran. He observed with interest the religious dimension of the protest movement, and was greatly impressed by the will of the ordinary Iranians for a change of administration. On an intellectual level, he was very interested in the nature of revolution and its capacity to challenge established political power. During October the Ayatollah Khomeini was expelled from Iran because of his political activities and was accepted for residence in France. In January 1979 the gathering political unrest forced the Shah to leave Iran, and two weeks later, on 1 February, the Ayatollah returned to Teheran, to huge welcoming crowds. It did not take long, however, before bitter reprisals and executions of former associates of the Shah's regime started to take place. Foucault was clearly taken aback by the actions of the new regime, though he did not substantially amend his earlier analysis of the morality of the Iranian Revolution.

Foucault's experience of the political events in Iran reflected an essential dichotomy in his thinking, an issue which had in one form or another, occupied him for most of his life. What is the key factor that determines the kind of life we lead?

For the immediate post-war generation who had experienced the German occupation of France, and the deprivations of World War II, the answer echoed around the streets of the Latin Quarter in Paris: Make of life what you will! Choose your own destiny!

Jean-Paul Sartre (1905–80) had said that existence precedes essence. In other words, when we are born, there is no sense in which our potential is limited. We exist, and we are free to determine the essence of what we will become. This notion of human freedom, central to the philosophy of **existentialism**, chimed perfectly with the mood of the time. The freedom of Europe had been restrained for so long that people longed to be told that they were free to determine their own destiny. No longer need they take account of external constraints; they could make their own choices.

Insight

Existentialism, which emphasized the freedom of individuals, had a lasting influence over subsequent decades and played an important role in shaping the ideas of the 1960s and 1970s 'liberation' movements, notably feminism and gay rights.

However, in the post-war years, the social and political situation changed. Enormous economic expansion occurred in France during the 'thirty glorious years' of 1945 to 1975. A new constitution in 1958 brought the start of the Fifth Republic, and President de Gaulle influenced many of the developments that saw the growth of the European Economic Community (EEC). The key political policy was *dirigisme,* or centralized state control, coupled with a measure of capitalism. Foucault lived through this period of increasing state control and intervention in society. It is perhaps no coincidence that he, in opposition to Sartre's world view, stressed the influence of the structures of society in determining the lives of individual human beings.

Insight

According to Foucault, the individual identity is not self-determining. The subjective self does not exist because of the free will and autonomy of the individual. Rather our identity is created through a system of socialization over which we have relatively little control. We are born into a particular social setting, a political system, a society with a particular set of values, and a religious system. All of these conspire to forge and mould our subjectivity. The individual looks out at the world with a vision that tends to reflect the surrounding ideological system.

In early 1983 Foucault again visited California to give a series of lectures, but from time to time he felt unwell, and when he returned to Paris he commenced a series of hospital treatments. He developed a series of symptoms that would now probably be associated with AIDS, although in the early 1980s the infection was little understood. Michel Foucault died on 25 June 1984. the French Socialist Prime Minister at the time, Pierre Mauroy (1928–), described Foucault as 'one of the great French contemporary philosophers'.

10 THINGS TO REMEMBER

1 *Foucault belonged to a long academic tradition, becoming a professor at the Collège de France.*

2 *At university in Paris, he was known for his unconventional behaviour.*

3 *At the Ecole normale supérieure he studied under the Marxist philosopher Louis Althusser.*

4 *In 1951 Foucault became a member of the French Communist Party.*

5 *In the 1950s Foucault was made Director of the French Cultural Centre in Warsaw.*

6 *He wrote about the 'archaeology' of knowledge, signifying the examination of the way in which different systems of thought are characteristic of different historical periods.*

7 *In 1968 Foucault became the first Professor of Philosophy at the Experimental University Centre of Vincennes.*

8 *In 1970 he founded the Groupe d'information sur les prisons (GIP), which acted as a pressure group for prison reform.*

9 *In 1975 he was a visiting professor at the University of California, Berkeley.*

10 *He died in Paris in 1984.*

2

The excavation of knowledge

In this chapter you will learn about:
* *Foucault's concept of the history and development of knowledge*
* *his analysis of the key intellectual features that characterized the main historical periods*
* *Foucault's notion of 'discourse' and the manner in which it influences our understanding of the world.*

The development of knowledge

Foucault was very interested in the history of knowledge, but not in a conventional sense. The history of knowledge has often been thought of as a series of events such as discoveries, inventions and journeys across previously uncharted areas. It was not, however, in this sense that Foucault perceived the history of knowledge. He was interested, first, in the way in which a particular set of ideas or a world view was pre-eminent for a long period of time, only to be replaced, either gradually or suddenly, by a different set of ideas. Secondly, he was also interested in the way in which concepts change over a long time period. While the word used to represent a concept may not change, the idea or ideas represented by the concept certainly do change. In other words, Foucault was less interested in the facts associated with the changes in knowledge, as with the mechanisms and processes by which our understanding of the world alters. Moreover, he saw ideological systems as exerting great influence over our ideas, and was interested in the way in which one belief system becomes liberated from one ideology, only to find itself later constrained by a different ideology. Foucault observed that history is often presented as a series of facts or events, completely dissociated from the nature of human society, and yet for him history was always firmly embedded in the thoughts and perceptions of human beings. As history was a human creation, it was subject to different interpretations at different times.

Insight

In Foucault's view, historical events are seen as a social construction, rather than as disembodied facts. For example, when someone is removed from power, it is not seen as a specific event at a particular time, but as the product of a complex interaction between human beings. Quite apart from the event itself, the manner in which it is perceived is also understood as a social interpretation. History is seen as a series of social interactions, rather than isolated events.

Much of human intellectual endeavour has been concerned with an attempt to understand the nature of historical development in purely rational terms. In other words, scholars have tried to understand the development of history by explaining it as a logical, sequential process that ultimately could lead to a more complete appreciation of the human condition. Foucault challenged the possibility of such a rational analysis, seeing history as much more unpredictable. Foucault's analyses concerning knowledge in general are contained in *Les Mots et les choses: une archéologie des sciences humaines* (1966), published in English as *The Order of Things: An archaeology of the human sciences* (1970); and also *L'Archéologie du savoir* (1969), published in English as *The Archaeology of Knowledge* (1972).

Foucault described his study of the history of knowledge as 'archaeology', an apt metaphor to refer to his efforts to gradually reveal the layers of human understanding that had existed in different epochs. One of Foucault's interesting suggestions was that human beings do not specifically and intentionally create systems of thought. Rather, the latter are a product of the activities of human beings. In other words, particular ways of acting or thinking presuppose a specific pattern of knowledge, which then becomes characteristic of a particular historical period.

The nature of the episteme

In each historical period, according to Foucault, there evolved a consensus about the underlying principles that govern the creation of valid knowledge. When people arrive at a consensus that something is true, they do so within the boundaries of certain principles. The latter are the intellectual rules that for that period of history controlled the process of establishing valid knowledge. Foucault gave the sum total of these rules the name **episteme**.

A key problem for Foucault, however, was to try to explain how one episteme could give way to another. If in one historical period we assume the existence of certain epistemological rules, then these would presumably govern the ways in which human beings think. If this is true, then it is difficult to understand how people could break out of this episteme to think in a completely different way. This is one of the logical problems created by the notion of the episteme. Perhaps one way of resolving the problem would be to consider the existence, in every age, of individuals who refuse to conform to the accepted way of thinking about the world. Such people create their own rules and, in so doing, often persuade others to follow them. Their influence can often become widespread and give rise to new ways of looking at the world – in other words, a new episteme. Perhaps Foucault himself was one such person.

Insight

The transformation of one episteme to another can often be a very challenging or even violent process. If we think of the major historical revolutionary periods, such as the French Revolution, when existing perceptions of the world were fundamentally challenged, we can see that they were often accompanied by significant structural changes in society.

Foucault reflected upon the principal periods of human intellectual development and attempted to identify the key features of the episteme characteristic of that period. In the **Renaissance period,** Foucault argued that human beings typically tried to understand the world and the universe by making connections between things. Astrological observations and their alleged connections with life on earth would be typical of this world view. The positions of the stars and planets were considered to be connected to human personality or to events in the lives of people. There was no apparent rationality or logic in the making of such connections, but merely the idea that it seemed probable that there should be some connection.

Within our modern scientific view of the world, such apparently random connections seem extremely improbable and unscientific, yet within the prevalent episteme of the Renaissance they were perfectly acceptable. In fact, they were rendered more plausible by the extremely theocentric view of the universe prevalent at the time. If one saw, as was the case in the Renaissance, that God controlled everything in the universe, then it became relatively straightforward to see connections between apparently disparate entities. After all, if God created everything, then a connection between two things was simply a connection between two of God's creations. There was thus a certain logic within this episteme, although it was not a logic that we would find particularly acceptable today.

Insight

Within a particular episteme there is a system of coherent logic that makes sense to all those *within* the episteme. It is, in a sense, a closed social and **epistemological** system that has its own intrinsic logic. *Outside* the episteme, the internal logic may appear less coherent.

One of the features of this episteme was that some writers and thinkers would find new connections that they would argue were significant for humanity. This gave rise to sometimes obscure and complex schools of thought, including the development of varieties of mystical knowledge. It was often difficult for others to challenge the validity of such knowledge systems because there were essentially no established grounds upon which one could challenge an intellectual system. One could only say that it contravened an existing system of thought, and hence was unacceptable. In the strongest example of such an argument, one could classify a new thought system as being in opposition to the teachings of the church, and hence heretical. This was, at the time, the most powerful means of suppression of a new thought system.

Foucault argued, however, that the Renaissance episteme was gradually replaced by that of what he termed the **classical** period, founded upon a more rational system of thought. There were already in the Renaissance age challenges to the irrationality of creating 'knowledge' simply by connection. People were beginning to take measurements of the world around them, and to employ such quantification to reflect upon, and indeed to challenge, the prevailing episteme. The measurement of the world provided a logical basis for the new episteme of the classical period. There were now grounds upon which knowledge could be tested. A proposition could be supported or challenged depending upon the extent to which it was consistent with mathematical logic.

Measurement enabled the world to be categorized. Objects could be classified into groups or into sequences, depending upon such characteristics as size. Mathematics could give such classifications a precise basis in measurement. One could now say that Object A was larger than Object B, or that Object C was higher in a rank order than Object D. These propositions now had an objectivity that was previously absent. Relationships between objects could now be determined, not on the basis of intuition, but on the basis of objective measurement. Objects could be grouped together or categorized on the basis of criteria such as size, width, velocity or mass – criteria that could be evaluated objectively. Moreover, such criteria were of general or universal application. They could be applied to the stars and planets, as well as to small objects on earth.

However, as Foucault pointed out, there was a further consequence of this revolution in the approach to knowledge. In the Renaissance period, human beings were at the epicentre of the concept of the nature of knowledge. They interpreted the universe and were the source of the links and connections that established an understanding of the natural and spiritual world. However, once there existed independent, objective criteria for assessing knowledge, the pre-eminence of humanity was no longer assured. Human beings were simply a part of this wider scientific universe. Human beings could be evaluated, compared and analysed in a similar way to anything else in the universe.

Insight

With the classical episteme, according to Foucault, there was a profound transformation in the way human beings were perceived. The latter were now part of the classification of the natural world, and subject to the same biological and scientific forces as other living creatures.

If the classical period tended to reduce the significance of human beings, the **Modern** period generated a different episteme that upgraded their significance in a different way. Foucault argued that in the nineteenth century a new episteme developed that was characterized by a new analysis of the social, economic and political factors that helped create contemporary society. As human society was the principal object of these enquiries, human beings once again became the central subject matter in attempts to explain and understand the world.

Philosophers and sociologists became interested in the way in which power, authority and control were distributed in society. They sought to explain the processes whereby some people could gain economic and political power, while other social groups appeared to have little influence. They were interested in the way wealth was distributed in society, and in the mechanisms of social mobility. They wanted to analyse the social mechanisms by which society changed, and to try to analyse the question of whether society was tending to evolve in any particular direction. There were also questions of social stratification and the processes whereby these social strata developed. In short, the concern of

the episteme of the Modern period was with the multifarie
social processes that made society what it was. As these proce.
were intimately involved with the actions and approaches of
human beings, the latter were once again placed at the centre of
philosophical debate.

Insight

An additional characteristic of the Modern episteme is
that the methods of science can also be used to investigate
human society. Theories concerning the way in which
society operates can be analysed and subjected to a process
of verification or falsification using the methods of scientific
enquiry.

The individual and society

A fundamental question for Foucault was whether there are
actual social structures that really exist and which consequently
have a controlling influence upon the lives of human beings. As
an example, one might take the issue of social class. We could
envisage social classes as actual strata in society into which we
are born and live our lives. On this view, there are actual social
divisions, and each class has its own characteristics, and its own
economic and political systems of thought. If this is an accurate
picture of society, then these social structures are able to influence
the lives of people, and it is difficult for the individual to escape
their influence. This viewpoint is known as **structuralism.**

However, we need not necessarily accept this view of the
pre-eminence of structures in human society. Instead, we could
perceive the individual as the creator of his or her own destiny.
On this model, real social structures do not exist in society, but
rather each individual creates his or her vision of the social world.
The problem with this view, however, is that each person tends to
be unwilling to accept the value of the macro social or economic
systems that have the capacity to act as a unifying force in society.

Foucault always tended to resist the idea that he was a structuralist. Indeed he did not appear to agree with the role of the intellectual as involving the creation of new macro world views to replace existing ones. Rather he considered that it was the role of the philosopher or thinker, to analyse and expose to view and to critique the functioning of society. What was important according to Foucault was to enable everyone to be able to understand the mechanisms by which economic, political and social power are distributed in society. Using this information, people would then be able to make up their own minds concerning the type of political system they wished to support.

Later in his life, Foucault studied Zen Buddhism in Japan. A strong element in the nature of Buddhist meditation is to live in the present moment, and not to be too concerned with future events or with the larger scheme of things. Foucault perhaps found some support in Buddhism for his own view that the intellectual should not be too concerned with developing, large-scale philosophical systems of thought. The philosophy of Buddhism tends to concentrate on the ordinary process of day-to-day living and to try to understand something of the way the mind approaches and responds to the nature of existence.

Insight

Foucault became familiar with the training regimes found in Buddhist monasteries. These are characterized by an emphasis on routine manual work as a way of meditating and learning to live in the present. The trainee monk is encouraged to focus on the present moment and not to become concerned with either the past or the future.

Certainly Foucault does appear to have provided a different model of the intellectual to that traditionally encountered in European philosophy and intellectual life. Marx provided a macro analysis of the mechanisms of society, and the key economic factors which he saw as determining both the nature of society and historical development. Jean-Paul Sartre, with whom Foucault is often contrasted, also provided a sweeping analysis of the nature of human existence, and the way in which he considered human beings should lead their lives. Foucault, however, in his research and writing often examined isolated historical events, and tried to show what we could learn from such events about the nature of society at that time.

Insight

In terms of research methodology, one might describe Foucault's approach as a 'case study method'. While this provides a detailed picture of a specific instance of something, and although the data may be rich and informative, it is not always easy to generalize from these specific cases and draw more general conclusions.

The concept of discourse

In his studies of the nature of knowledge, Foucault also became very interested in the contribution of **discourse** to the way in which we approach and understand the world. In *The Order of Things*, he defined discourse as 'representation itself, represented by verbal signs' (p. 81). He argued that there was an identifiable and distinguishable mode of discourse for each of the institutions and sectors of society. For example, in the workplace normal discourse is characterized typically by discussion of concepts such as workloads, salary levels, customer satisfaction, delivery deadlines and financial viability. It is concepts such as these which are woven together and integrated into a discourse typical of the workplace. Such a discourse functions in a number of different ways. It enables us, for example, to identify when we are in a work context. When we are at work, and perhaps engaged in social conversation with colleagues, we are able to recognize immediately when the discourse has changed to one involving work issues. The nature of the concepts being used changes, and we are immediately aware that we are talking in a different way and, in effect, using a different form of discourse.

Moreover, the nature of the reasoning process and logic is transformed from one discourse to another. When we are engaged in social conversation at work, the discourse is characterized by emotive arguments, feelings, attitudes and the expression of preferences. For example, we might be comparing views about a film we have seen, and different colleagues will express their views as to whether they thought it was well acted or whether the film had a good script. Essentially, the discourse will be characterized by the expression of opinions. On the other hand, if the conversation changes to one involving work issues, the discourse will be more frequently characterized by the discussion of bureaucratic procedures, by an evaluation of legal or regulatory systems, or by an analysis of economic or fiscal systems. The nature of the discourse will be more formal, and will be related to trying to ensure that employment-related systems proceed efficiently and effectively.

There are many other forms of discourse characteristic of different subject disciplines, different institutions in society, and different contexts. A scientific discourse is characterized by the existence of **empirical** evidence, which is analysed and evaluated in order to generate general statements such as hypotheses and theories. A family has a different mode of discourse from a sports club, or from an academic institution. Each has a mode of discourse that is related to the concepts and ideas typically associated with the context, and also a discourse that reflects the goals and purposes of that context.

Additionally, however, the mode of discourse of an institution or context is also very much connected to both the type of knowledge that is considered legitimate and valid in that context, and also to the type of knowledge that can in theory be generated. For example, the family is an institution concerned in part with moral knowledge. One of its main functions is to socialize young children into modes of behaviour that are not only ethical in principle but which also conform to the accepted values of society. Moreover, the family can also help children to generate moral knowledge by encouraging them to test out behaviour patterns for themselves and to evaluate the consequences in terms of morality.

This is but one function of the discourse characteristic of the family, and it happens also to be one that is associated with academic institutions such as schools. They, too, are concerned with the transmission of moral understanding. In addition, however, they are also concerned with the transmission of empirical knowledge, as in physics or biology, and also with means of communication such as the use of foreign languages or information technology. The style of discourse in relation to educational understanding often involves such concepts as achievement levels, literacy, assessment, performance and standards.

It is part of the skill of a competent, socialized individual to be able to move from one mode of discourse to another with fluency. Such a person can then operate easily in different social contexts. There are, however, some forms of societal discourse that are characterized by complex terminology, and which it is frequently difficult for the layperson to understand. Such discourses are often associated with powerful and influential professions such as medicine. One consequence of this is that, while it permits members of, say, the medical profession to communicate with each other effectively, the patient or other layperson cannot necessarily understand the nature and meaning of the discourse and is therefore excluded from participation. This permits the medical practitioner to exercise his or her power and influence in a way that remains relatively unchallenged by others. He or she can take decisions, draw conclusions, or recommend treatments, without anyone other than another member of the profession being able to challenge their authority and judgement. Discourse can thus be very much associated with power and with the ability to exercise that power.

Insight

Discourse is not only related to power in terms of specialist vocabulary. Discourse also helps to define a particular type of person as suitable to have power and authority over others. It helps to define where exactly power will be located, and it acts as an advocate of power, helping to inform and persuade the majority of citizens to accept the exercise of power in certain ways, and not in others.

Medical discourse enables doctors to retain a sense of exclusivity of knowledge in the profession, yet in recent years this has to some extent been challenged by access to the Internet. The layperson can now have access to the full range of medical knowledge in a form of discourse that is much more understandable by the non-expert. To some extent, all professions use their own discourse as a means of exercising control and power over their clients and over the decision-making process. This is to a degree true of law, accountancy, education and the scientific and technical professions. Nevertheless, through the intervention of the Internet, society is experiencing a democratization of knowledge and its increased accessibility to members of the public. One can only wonder at how Foucault would have reacted to this revolution.

Discourse as power and knowledge is also very evident among those who as politicians, control society. We all have personal views about the way in which politicians discuss and debate issues, and ultimately pass on their decisions to the electorate. However, one could argue that one feature of such discourse is often a lack of precision. Politicians are often asked to state what actions they will take in the future, yet are often characteristically vague about what that will be. They know all too well that economic and social conditions can change rapidly, and to predict exactly a course of action may not be totally appropriate. Politicians will often tend to leave themselves the maximum flexibility of action, and this can lead to a form of discourse that is characterized by a certain lack of precision.

Foucault was interested in the way in which different modes of discourse are associated with particular periods in history. Indeed, he saw history to some extent as being the study of different modes of discourse, and he referred to this as the study of **genealogy**. He wrote of discourse as 'all that remains is representation, unfolding in the verbal signs that manifest it, and hence becoming discourse' (*The Order of Things*, p. 79). In the sense that discourse is a reflection of the different forms of culture, customs and, indeed, knowledge, then discourse is typical of a particular historical period. Moreover, there is a close relationship between the discourse typical of a historical period, and the type of knowledge characteristic of that era.

Insight

Discourse also helps to create history. If a form of discourse defines another nation as politically friendly, then a variety of consequences will follow from that, including economic, trade and cultural links. History will thus evolve in parallel with the predominant discourse.

Foucault was interested in discourse as a phenomenon, at least partly because of its relationship to knowledge and power. For Foucault, power – and those who exercised it – had the capacity to create large-scale systems of thought that could exert considerable influence over people's lives. He always appeared to be against such systems of control, and hence sought to expose the nature of power and to limit its influence over people. It was necessary for Foucault to work continually to understand power, and to analyse its mode of functioning. Nevertheless, Foucault was reluctant to topple one system of power only to replace it with his own. He did not wish to assume the role of an advocate for any particular ideological system, and throughout his life he tried to avoid advocating a large-scale view of the way in which people should live. Nevertheless, we shall examine later in the book the ways in which Foucault tried to engage politically in order to assist those individuals and groups whom he viewed as victims of the exercise of power.

Foucault, however, came under much criticism for failing to provide an alternative ideology that could be a realistic substitute for what some perceived as the unfairness and inequalities of the prevalent capitalist system of liberal economics. Foucault's critics pointed out, while he recognized the inadequacies of the West's economic system, he would not propose an alternative. His reluctance to do this could be at least partly explained by his wish to avoid replacing one form of power by another.

10 THINGS TO REMEMBER

1   *Foucault was very interested in the mechanisms by which knowledge systems change during different historical periods.*

2   *He considered that ideologies in society greatly affect the lives of individuals.*

3   *History for Foucault was very much connected with the nature of human thought in different periods.*

4   *Each historical period possesses a set of intellectual rules, the 'episteme', which are used to establish valid knowledge.*

5   *Foucault tried to establish the nature of the episteme for different historical periods.*

6   *Foucault is often thought of as a structuralist, although he denied this – he did not appear to like labels of any kind being attached to him.*

7   *He did not wish to replace one sort of power with another, but rather to help people understand the nature of power in society.*

8   *The discourse of a particular profession is partly responsible for sustaining the power of that profession.*

9   *Discourse was seen by Foucault as a key element in the creation of power in society.*

10   *Foucault was criticized for not developing on alternative system to liberal capitalism.*

3

....

The nature of power

In this chapter you will learn about:
- *Foucault's perceptions of the student protests of May 1968*
- *his views of power during different historical periods*
- *the ways in which power operates, according to Foucault, in a postmodern society.*

Power and the education system

The student protests of May 1968 may have seemed on one level to have been a failure. Many of those picking up stones to throw or overturning cars to form barricades may have thought that a form of workers' control, or of left-wing radical government, was about to be created. The power of the Gaullist administration was, if anything, reinforced – almost by virtue of its evident capacity to withstand the concerted opposition shown by workers' groups and students. Nevertheless, as Foucault realized, the real success of 1968 was not in the revolutionary exercise of governmental power, but in the revolution in the minds of ordinary French citizens. After 1968 people in France, and to a certain extent in the rest of the world, were open to ideas that they would not previously have even considered.

The events of 1968 were in a sense 'iconic' and were influential in many Western countries. The change in power relations was the real consequence of 1968 – not in administration, government, or the great institutions of State, but, in a sense, in the thought processes of the electorate at the micro level. Foucault appreciated this, and it may have been one reason why, in the years after 1968, he began to participate more and more in politics. This was not, however, the politics of the political party or of the democratic process, but of the pressure group – the politics of micro-societal change that sometimes managed to influence the State on a larger scale.

Insight

Foucault grasped the idea that the exercise of power was not necessarily about the overthrow of institutions, organizations, bureaucracies, or indeed the State. The exercise of true power was much more about the redistribution of influence and the ability to change the way people thought. Then, given time, and the appropriate circumstances, it was possible that institutions would be changed, too.

Ideas changed after 1968, and nowhere more so than in education. The events of 1968 were largely brought about initially by students. It is true that it was also a workers' revolution, but the ideas came largely from students, participants in the education system. One notable feature of this change in the way people viewed the education system was that many of the leading intellectuals who influenced it were the product of the conventional education system. Foucault, Sartre, Simone de Beauvoir (1908–86) and Raymond Aron (1905–1983) had been educated within the formal French system. They had studied the canonical texts specified by the higher education curriculum and were well versed in traditional philosophy and sociology. Yet even though they had been educated within this curricular framework they realized its limitations. They understood that it was restrictive in the barriers that it tended to place on thought, and yet because of the strength of their intellects they were able to go beyond the limitations that it placed upon them.

Prior to 1968 those who were 'educated' were able to exercise a degree of power and influence in society by virtue of having mastered a body of knowledge. Those who were able to manipulate ideas skilfully, to combine ideas from different sources, possessed elements of power purely derived from this capacity. And yet this was a skill, an ability, and not really a quality that gave them the capacity to look at the world in a different way. The events of 1968 gave people the capacity to take traditional ideas and to use them to think about the world differently, and indeed to advocate changes. The idea of using education to change social structures and social relations represented a major transformation of power relations. Henceforth students would be taught that their role was not merely to acquire knowledge in a passive way, but to use it to find ways to alter society for the better. In practical terms, this tended to alter the relationship between lecturers and students. Lecturers encouraged students to take traditional knowledge and to interpret it in their own way, not merely to replicate the opinions of their teachers.

Insight

After 1968 the Western education system became much more empowering and teachers were able to talk about the transformative function of education. Although many aspects of the formal university curriculum would remain, new courses in the humanities and social sciences appeared, together with newer forms of assessment.

Foucault was intrinsically in harmony with this position because he consistently tried to avoid adopting a narrow ideological position on issues and passing this on to his students. He would often not respond to questions from either students or journalists that implicitly invited him to assume a particular intellectual position. He much preferred to outline the evidence relevant to an issue, and then to invite his questioner to formulate his or her own ideas. This type of approach to teaching represented a major transformation of power, and could be found throughout the educational systems of the West after 1968, at all levels from schools to higher education.

In science teaching, for example, it became an accepted process to encourage students to experiment freely in the laboratory, rather than having them repeat classical 'experiments'. In harmony with the nature of the scientific thought process, the teaching process became much more truly exploratory. Pupils in schools were invited to develop scientific ideas from first principles, rather than simply learning traditional scientific procedures. The decade following 1968 also saw the rise of subjects such as sociology, the latter providing a vehicle for students to reflect upon the very nature of the society that was changing so rapidly.

Insight

During the post-1968 period there were also challenges to the very nature of the formal state-school itself. Radical writers around the world, for example Ivan Illich in his book *Deschooling Society* (1971), challenged some of the accepted principles of schooling, and called for entirely new principles of education to be developed and applied.

The approach of this period was to make education as far as possible 'student-centred', although this did beg the question of what exactly was intended by the word 'centred'. In some ways it implied that students had a measure of control over what they studied, and to a certain extent this was true. Teachers and lecturers did still control the curriculum in a formal sense, but types of assessment were changing. There was a rapidly evolving change from the use of formal examinations to assignments and project work. The latter provided students with considerable freedom and represented a major movement of power from the teacher and lecturer to the student. The use of formal examinations as a type of assessment gave teachers the means to compare students more precisely and hence to be able to place them in a rank order of success. However, the increased use of project work made it more problematic to compare students, and hence it became more usual to avoid a hierarchical ranking of student performance.

The actual structure of the teaching process also changed. There was a gradual move away from formal lectures, from the taking of notes by students and the expectation that students should be able to reproduce those notes. Classrooms became much more frequently places in which groups of students worked together on assignments, and where the teacher acted much more as an organizer of the learning process, rather than as transmitter of facts. The teacher had formerly been viewed as a repository of knowledge, or as a subject expert, but was now seen much more as a facilitator of the educational process – someone who assisted students in the organization of their own learning.

Insight

Foucault was an important influence on the development of student-centred education and thus helped make possible the transition to the mass system of university education we know today. Without the newer approaches to learning, and importantly the more innovative approaches to assessment, it would probably not have been possible to accommodate so many students in the higher education system.

Central to this change in the nature of education was a change in the nature of discourse. For Foucault, as we saw in Chapter 2, discourse was fundamentally connected to the nature of power. Those who had the power to influence the nature of discourse exerted considerable control over the nature of the educational system and the manner in which people thought about the world. Foucault had considerable doubts about the validity of teaching people what they should think. He appears to have far preferred to encourage his students to think for themselves. This indeed is reflected for Foucault in the nature of the discourse used, which after 1968 was much more closely related to **Socratic dialogue**. Instead of students being 'told' that something was true, they were invited to consider the logical consequences of certain forms of evidence. Students were thus invited to observe the empirical world, to record their observations, and then to draw systematic conclusions. The latter might involve, for example, the generation of hypotheses or of provisional theories. Students would, in addition, be asked to suggest general propositions about the world, and then to indicate examples of evidence that might be useful in determining the veracity or otherwise of such statements. For Foucault, this type of discourse was very significant in terms of power, because it encouraged young people to create their own vision of truth in the world, rather than being told what they should believe.

Power and the state

To a degree Foucault was probably not surprised that there
was no major shift of political power after 1968, since he had
already noted the diffuse nature of power in the modern State.
Foucault argued that power was in effect distributed among the
many institutions and organizations of the State. Political and
economic power resided partly with elected politicians, partly with
the civil service, with banks and industrial corporations, partly
with the army, the police, the legal system, and with many other
aspects of society. This extensive network of power could not be
replaced merely by virtue of a few student demonstrations. Power
of this type was too dispersed and too difficult to challenge. It
might be possible to mount a challenge against one aspect of it,
but in totality it permeated too much of society to be effectively
addressed.

Nevertheless the events of 1968 did lay down an effective challenge
of a different kind, and that was in terms of discourse. The student
rebels on the streets during May 1968 may not have realized that
this was what was happening, but the aftermath showed that the
most powerful challenge to authority came through a challenge to
existing ideas. It came through a challenge to the thought processes
of men and women, and the way in which they looked at the world.

Foucault argued that in society there is an inescapable connection
between power and knowledge. Power requires knowledge to
be effective, and knowledge, at the same time, generates power.

For example, a knowledge of the legal system of a state enables one to argue what is entitled and permitted to happen. Events and explanations can be effectively challenged if one understands the rules by which circumstances are judged. Our education system also provides access to power. In the most direct way, an education system provides access to specialized knowledge, which thus helps to determine who is viewed as an 'expert' or specialist in society. However, in a more subtle way, an education system gives access to a mode of thinking that enables those who are effectively introduced to this mode of discourse to determine whether something can be considered as true or false. Those who are included within the academic mode of discourse are able, for example, to determine the type of data that is acceptable when addressing a particular question.

Academics understand through their training not only what type of data should be collected, but what type of methodology should be employed to collect it. They are trained how then to analyse the data and, importantly, how to draw conclusions from the analysis. They also appreciate that, in drawing conclusions, they should not exceed the limits of their data. In other words, they should not draw conclusions that exceed what is reasonable, and what may be logically derived from their data. In this way they do not make truth claims that are excessive or that would leave them open to criticism by colleagues. The ability to make reasonable claims, and only those claims that can be effectively supported, is a form of power derived from a knowledge of academic procedures.

Insight

Rational academic authority can be extremely influential, in that it enables individuals to marshal arguments using logic and systematic discussion. This type of dialogue has the capacity to change people's opinions, and, as Foucault pointed out, power of this kind can, in the long term, be very influential.

Power in different historical periods

The dispersed system of power found in modern societies contrasts with that evident in many ancient societies. There power usually tended to reside in one person and was extremely localized and unitary in nature. During a period of internal revolution or of external assault, it was normally only necessary to depose the single ruler to gain control of the state. However, as societies became more complex, so did systems of government, and with the modern period came sophisticated and devolved models of power. It therefore became much more difficult to take control of a state. In former times power was normally linked to an aristocracy that was able to control the lives of the less influential social classes. In the modern period, however, some types of power, influence and authority became delegated to those classes that in previous periods had possessed no power. For example, in the modern age, industrial production became an enormous factor in the economic power possessed by a state, and hence the mass of workers who generated that industrial production possessed, de facto, political power. It was in part Marx's explanation of economic relationships that awakened industrial workers to the potential of their position and enabled them to realize and wield, through mechanisms such as the trade union movement, their political power.

Foucault draws an interesting contrast between the nature of the individual in medieval societies, and that of the individual in modern, industrial societies. He also comments upon the nature of the power which they possess. In the medieval period there was in principle a relatively highly individualized concept of the person. People could act in a manner that identified them as different. In the modern period, however, there was a greater tendency for people to be organized, to be placed in categories, to be regularized, and to act as a group rather than as an individual. The paradigmatic case would be, for example, the industrial working classes who might be allocated numbers rather than names and have to submit to mechanisms for time control at the beginning and end of their period of work. In time-and-motion studies, the individual's mode of functioning at work is subdivided and analysed into very small elements of actions. Such approaches to work de-individualize the person, and reduce their power and influence as individuals. As mentioned above, the only power they can exert under such systems is the collective power of the economic group.

Foucault drew attention to the power exercised by those who are able to observe people and to pass judgements on them in a modern industrial society. In the case above, for example, the time-and-motion expert is able to define an individual worker as efficient or inefficient, and this can determine their progress within the hierarchy of the work environment, their remuneration and indeed the esteem in which they are held in the workplace. Foucault argued that observation and monitoring of the individual is not only one of the key characteristics of contemporary life but also one of the principal means by which power is exercised.

We are all observed, argued Foucault, in a wide variety of situations. Our weight and height are monitored as babies and young children, and, as soon as we are able to attend school, our intellectual performance is carefully compared to that of our peers. Abilities at reading and basic numeracy are carefully assessed, and our progress evaluated and recorded. When we start work, our performance in the world of economic productivity is evaluated and records maintained. Just as the development of our powers and abilities is carefully observed when we are younger, when we are older the decline in our abilities is also carefully monitored. Our eyesight is checked to ensure we can continue to drive, and our medical condition in terms of blood pressure and cholesterol levels carefully recorded. It is difficult to avoid this incessant monitoring of our bodies and minds. For Foucault this is one of the major manifestations of power in the modern world. We are required to submit ourselves to this observation, and through a variety of complex and carefully controlled administrative mechanisms the State ensures that it is capable of carrying out this observation. Moreover, there are continual efforts to improve and extend the amount of observation and the thoroughness with which it takes place.

Foucault pointed out that enormous power accrues to those who conduct observations on individuals within society. The observer is able to define certain people as not complying with what might be expected of them in comparison with others. Those in authority can then define a regime of treatment for those who do not match the norms expected.

The computer age has provided the State with very effective mechanisms for monitoring and observing the individual. Whenever we visit a site on the Internet, this can be recorded, and our patterns of interests, purchases and explorations of knowledge can be analysed. Not only can this data be collected, but it may be passed on to commercial organizations for use in marketing and sales. Through the use of the mobile phone our movements can be traced, and our contacts and networks observed and monitored. The extension of the collection and deployment of biodata such as retinal scans and DNA extends the power of the State still further. Moreover, the increasing use of video cameras throughout society provides the State with the power to monitor our movements, including, not least, our driving patterns. All of these techniques represent an enormous expansion of State power to observe, monitor and control its citizens, and thereby develop strategies to control the ways in which people behave.

Foucault also argued that through the use of these techniques there was a tendency for the individual to be rendered more and more passive and malleable. The awareness of this extensive power of the state to observe the individual gives a sense of powerlessness to the extent that the individual feels little freedom for movement or decision-making. Everything appears controlled by the state's bureaucratic system, and in the face of this there is a tendency to assume that the individual human being has little freedom of action, little autonomy and little power over their lives.

We have already seen how Foucault was interested in the ways in which power permeated society. Although he acknowledged that state power is important, he was more interested in power as a phenomenon that spreads throughout society with an almost innumerable range of foci. Power is, according to Foucault, visible and functioning at the micro level all the time. Foucault, however, went further than this in his analysis and pointed out that power was an intrinsic element of all human relations. At the lowest denominator of human relationships, in for example discourse between two people, a power differential would inevitably develop. One individual would influence the other in some respects, while in others power would flow in the reverse direction. Power was, according to Foucault, an element in all human relationships, and certainly in the workplace. It was however, he argued, not localized simply in the hierarchical structures of the work relationship, such as the power that resides in a head of department to determine the work functions of employees in that department. Power relations also exist between ordinary workers, and these power relationships work upwards in the hierarchy, affecting work patterns above them, just as power also works downwards through the hierarchy.

Insight

An *explanation* of the mechanisms through which power works in society does nothing to redistribute power. What is needed, some may say, is a *means of altering* some of the unfairness of the distribution of power in the world.

For example, it is difficult, if not impossible, for an administrator or manager higher up in a hierarchy to manage those below, and exert power over their working lives, if the workers do not accept the legitimacy of that authority and power. Power can only be effectively exerted if people accept the legitimate right of someone to exert power. Even in a strict hierarchy, it is difficult to exert power if people refuse to accept this legitimacy. As many managers discover to their cost, workers can find numerous strategies to foil managerial plans if they wish to do so, and those strategies may be all the more effective if they remain within the broad regulatory system of the organization. 'Working to rule' is a classical example of this strategy.

Power is thus also opposed. Even the most effective systems of power encompass people who will resist and oppose their ability to exercise power. This takes place as much in authoritarian societies and organizations as in liberal-democratic organizations. Moreover, just as power is very diffuse, opposition to power can arise in a great variety of different ways. In democratic organizations power is often exercised through committee structures, although the way in which committees are managed and organized may not be entirely democratic. In reality, the chair of the committee may exercise power in an autocratic manner. People can oppose the exercise of power through committees, but it may require that individuals are prepared to oppose those higher in a hierarchy and to accept that this may incur the displeasure of such people. Much of Michel Foucault's opposition to power took the form of collecting and disseminating information about an issue and then allowing a momentum to develop in the press and public opinion. For example, in his opposition to conditions in prison he set out to collect systematically as much data as possible on what was happening in prison, and then publicized this widely. The result was considerable counter-pressure on the government and prison authorities to improve the conditions within the prisons – conditions that, according to Foucault, caused prisoners to move 'deeper into criminality' (Gordon, *Michel Foucault: Power/Knowledge*, p. 40).

Insight

Foucault's research methodology was often very effective in terms of its sheer detail. The data he gathered on prison conditions, for example, was so impressive in its scope and depth that, when released into the public domain, it generated considerable momentum for change and reform.

The exercise of power

The idea of power was a concept that permeated much of Foucault's thinking. He viewed it as very much related to concepts of freedom, authority, subjection and resistance. He saw power as an aspect of an inter-relationship or interaction between human beings.

One person would have the capacity to influence another person, to influence their thinking, their behaviour, the people they choose as friends, and the way they conducted their lives. Nevertheless, according to Foucault, people did not necessarily submit to the exercise of power. They frequently resisted the exercise of power and showed that they were able to act with at least some autonomy. Of course, as Foucault pointed out, the exercise of power could seriously limit the actions of others, and restrict their freedom to act or to resist. Nevertheless, it appeared to be almost a characteristic feature of human beings that they should wish to exercise at least some degree of autonomy.

A very significant feature of the exercise of power is that those in a position of power and authority try to develop an intellectual justification for exercising that power. Even when a government or dictator wields a great deal of power and can, in effect, act completely autocratically, they will often, or even usually, try to *persuade* people that they are acting in the interests of the majority of citizens. Those in power will develop theories of society that purport to explain why one ethnic or cultural group is inferior to another; why one group should be persecuted, or why another group should remain economically deprived. Even powerful dictators appear not to want to act simply by virtue of the power they possess; rather they wish to be seen as virtuous leaders, perhaps having to take unpleasant decisions, but nevertheless decisions that are broadly necessary for the good of all.

So important, influential and all-pervasive are these ideologies of power that when combating the influence of power, it is more important to counteract the ideology than to fight force with force. It is a common assertion, with no doubt considerable validity, that a military victory alone is insufficient to combat a set of ideals or an ideology. A political or religious ideology can rarely be extinguished militarily. There are examples to the contrary, however, the Cathar philosophy in southern France in the Middle Ages being a case in point. This religious philosophy was regarded as heretical by the Roman Catholic Church, and was to all intents and purposes destroyed by the Albigensian Crusade (1209–29). Generally, however, such examples are relatively rare, and ideas seem to be more persistent than the exercise of military power and authority.

Foucault felt that the way in which power was exercised in society was generally unclear. Certainly there was evidence of some of the basic ways in which power was demonstrated, for example by the chief executive of a company or by a president or prime minister. Foucault, however, harboured the view that the true exercise of power was far more complex than this. It was more of a network of relationships than a simple vertical relationship within a hierarchy. The individuals who constitute society may sense that their lives are being regulated by a variety of institutions and social pressures, but in reality such forces are very difficult to define or to specify. Their influence, and indeed their power, permeates society and yet the individual person often has great difficulty in understanding exactly how their power operates. The exercise of power, according to Foucault, is hence very subtle and difficult to recognize, and operates by means of strategies that are difficult to identify.

Those who have worked in large organizations will be very familiar with decision-making in committees where it is often difficult to ascertain exactly how a particular decision is taken. The discussion will ebb and flow for a while, and there may be some direction from the chair, and gradually a decision will emerge. The process, in retrospect, may be difficult to describe. Equally, a decision may be arrived at in a committee, yet when the minutes are produced the decision may seem to have changed in a subtle way. No one suggests the minutes are inaccurate and hence the decision becomes confirmed. We are probably aware of many other analogous situations where decisions are taken in ways that are difficult to predict or to understand.

Not only is it, according to Foucault, a major problem to understand the manner in which power is exercised, but it is also very complex to develop an understanding of the way in which decisions become accepted as valid. For power to be exercised, it is often necessary that large numbers of people accept the legitimacy of the decision. Unless those people, often large numbers of people, are willing to accept a decision as valid, then such a decision cannot be effectively implemented.

There are also comparable situations in the health sector where limited resources are distributed to an ever more demanding group of consumers. Decisions have often to be made about the distribution and availability of scarce and expensive medication to patients with rare illnesses. Those with the power to take these decisions have to decide whether to provide sophisticated and costly medication to a few people, or whether to use the money to provide less expensive care for a larger number of patients suffering from a more routine condition. This draws to a focus one of the dilemmas of the exercise of state power. The state must be concerned with caring for the needs of the individual as well as it can, while at the same time ensuring that the broader concerns of the collectivity are catered for. These two competing demands may often be mutually incompatible. Individual needs may be specialized, calling for costly and complex provision, and they may inevitably remove resources from more straightforward provision. The exercise of power in making such decisions may often require that a campaign of publicity be undertaken to persuade the public of the validity of the decision.

Insight

In a **postmodern** society, where the majority of people have access to computers and the Internet, and other means of communication, ordinary citizens are well-equipped to challenge state decisions. Campaigns on public issues can be mounted very rapidly and can be a serious challenge to governmental authority.

Power, even in medieval times, has tended to be exercised only with the approval of the populace. For example, the ruler of a state, the king or queen, traditionally had a right over the life of the individual citizens of that state. However, this power could only be exercised under very limited circumstances. Normally, only if a citizen threatened the life of a monarch could the ruler demand the death penalty. The exercise of this right of execution could appear to be connected to the stability of the State, since this would be undermined if there was a likelihood of the monarch being assassinated. Of course, in other ways, the monarch might be able to place citizens in some potential danger. Under the feudal system, the feudal lord had the right to decide to wage war on another state perceived as an enemy, and under those circumstances to demand that their vassals take up arms on their behalf. Although this right to demand that the state wages war no longer accrues to a monarch in the modern state, it has nevertheless devolved to elected government representatives, to prime ministers and to presidents.

10 THINGS TO REMEMBER

1 *In May 1968 the stability of the government of President Charles de Gaulle was threatened by major student and worker protests.*

2 *At the start of the protests Foucault was living in Tunisia, working as a university lecturer.*

3 *Although Foucault had himself received a formal education, he supported many of the claims of the students for educational reform.*

4 *Foucault was seen by many as a focus for the demands for change.*

5 *After the events of 1968 there was considerable change in the curriculum of higher education.*

6 *The education system became considerably more student-centred.*

7 *Foucault noted the way in which observation of individuals was used to augment state power in the postmodern world.*

8 *He documented the relationship between power and the bureaucratic institutions of contemporary society.*

9 *Foucault appeared to have a natural reticence concerning advising people about adopting a particular ideology or world view.*

10 *He argued that power could only be exerted on people who wished to be placed in that position.*

4

The history of punishment

In this chapter you will learn about:
- *Foucault's analysis of changes in the types of judicial punishment characteristic of different historical periods*
- *his analysis of the potential reasons for some of these changes*
- *his views about the impact of different types of judicial punishment on the individual.*

The evolution of systems of punishment

One of Foucault's most celebrated studies is his exploration of the history of punishment – *Surveiller et punir: naissance de la prison* (1975; published in English as *Discipline and Punish: The birth of the prison* in 1977). He starts by looking back to the nature of punishment in the eighteenth century and before. He notes that in this period punishment was characterized by two principal features. First, it was extremely physical rather than psychological. It involved often extreme cruelties and torture, leading to an agonizing death. Secondly, this type of punishment was typically carried out publicly, and indeed appeared to be regarded by the general public as a form of entertainment. The authorities probably conducted such executions in public, partly as an attempt to bring justice into the public domain. People could be perfectly sure that a wrongdoer had received the punishment prescribed by law and would be dissuaded from ever doing something illegal themselves.

One may only hypothesize concerning the reasons for people wishing to watch such cruel spectacles. On the one hand, life in the eighteenth century and earlier was harsh, particularly for the social classes who were disadvantaged. Physical punishment may not have been quite as shocking to them as it would be to contemporary society, where we are used to a more 'civilized' life. Existence was more precarious because of the prevalence of disease, and people were perhaps more familiar with the imminence of death. Nevertheless, as Foucault pointed out, the prevalent philosophy of punishment entailed inflicting pain on the body.

The use of extreme forms of punishment during the eighteenth century and earlier ultimately received its justification from the sovereign of the state concerned. When a crime was committed, it was essentially not against society, but against the sovereign. The profound nature of such an act led to the justification of a broad range of unpleasant physical punishments. Although the punishment was considered as a public event to be watched and perhaps even enjoyed by the masses, there was also during the eighteenth century a developing opposition to such punishment. Living conditions for the majority of people were so adverse that there was a sense that state officials and ultimately the sovereign were self-serving rather than fulfilling responsibilities towards the populace. Hence when ordinary working-class people were ill-treated or executed for minor offences – often simply theft of food to assuage hunger – there was an evolving feeling of unfairness, leading ultimately to the seeds of social and political revolt. These kinds of feelings gave great support to those who considered it necessary to reform the system of punishment.

Insight

Foucault noted that public execution involving torture provided the kind of public spectacle to which the general populace rarely had access. On the other hand, he also observed that there was often a degree of public sympathy for the offender: the crowd would often shout offensive remarks directed at the government or others in authority for inflicting such a cruel punishment.

Towards the end of the eighteenth century, Foucault argued, the structure and nature of society began to change. Notably, society was becoming far more organized and regulated. In general, as we have already seen, citizens were subject to closer observation by administrative and quasi-governmental authorities. Incipient police forces were developed with the purpose of monitoring the citizenry, and placing in confinement anyone who might have transgressed. The greater organization of society led to a system of rules and regulation that permitted the citizen to know when they had transgressed, and the judiciary to assess accurately and objectively, the appropriate punishment.

There was also a changing sense of morality in society. Offences were seen rather less as crimes against government, authority or those in power, but rather more against the nature of society itself. A criminal offence was a crime against other citizens, against one's neighbours or community. Crime was a social offence and it was necessary for the punishment to be viewed as appropriate to the offence. There thus developed a social morality where different types of crime were viewed as more unethical than others.

Insight

Towards the end of the eighteenth century crimes began to be evaluated in terms of the extent of their negative effects on society, and the extent to which they reduced the cohesion of society. For instance, one element of such social cohesion was that people should work hard and gain from the proceeds of that hard work. Theft was seen to be serious because it undermined the advantages of hard work.

In the new social context of crime, citizens demanded a form of legal fairness in the evaluation of the likely guilt or innocence of someone. If this was not so, then an innocent person could easily be found guilty of a crime they did not commit. New rules and standards for the assessment of evidence were developed in order to be able to judge someone objectively and fairly. We are familiar in modern times with the way in which certain types of crime are grouped together and attract a comparable type of punishment.

So used are we to the logic of this type of judicial and legal system, that we perhaps take it for granted. Yet it was in the nineteenth century that we began to see the emergence of this type of system. The notion that 'the punishment should fit the crime' began to emerge as a rational system.

Foucault emphasized that 'detention and imprisonment do not form part of the European penal system before the great reforms of the years 1780–1820' (Rabinow, *Michel Foucault: Ethics*, p. 23). Superficially at least it seemed as if the tendency to move from physical punishment and torture as the basis of the system of punishment, to a system based upon imprisonment and perhaps psychological punishment, was more civilized and humane. For Foucault, however, this was not necessarily so. Taken as a whole, he appears to feel that the reforms constituted a much more systematic approach on the part of the state to organize a widespread and well-organized penal system and that it was a much more oppressive expression of power against the individual than the previous approach.

Insight

Public punishment, particularly through the use of torture, was essentially a form of punishment against the individual, and in particular a form of revenge on behalf of the state or the sovereign. However, the form of punishment that replaced it was more concerned with the imposition of authority on behalf of society, and with the control of that society.

The fundamental basis of the late eighteenth-century reforms was to be one of an apparent fairness in terms of the transparency of the functioning of the legal system. Punishments were re-evaluated to try to ensure that they were appropriate to the offence, and that they also acted as a deterrent to others. There were advantages in allocating the minimum punishment that would achieve these ends, since that would be also less economically burdensome to the state. The idea of the legal and judicial system was also linked to one of a police system. Society needed to be carefully and comprehensively observed in order that there was a high probability of an offender being detected and apprehended. There would be little use in an effective punishment system if no one could be caught to be punished.

There was also a developing interest in the nature of proof of guilt. In the early eighteenth century there had been a focus upon torture and physical punishment in order to persuade people to confess. In the newer system, the emphasis was now upon the employment of scientific, rational principles in the establishment of guilt or innocence. Data was systematically collected and evaluated, to be presented to the courts. In addition, there was a gradual realization that there was potentially a benefit to society to understand crime and the criminal. If the psychology of the criminal could be understood then there was a possibility that measures could be taken to reduce the levels of crime.

Insight

There was an increasing tendency from the late eighteenth century to try to understand the nature of human beings, both in a physical and psychological sense, employing the developing understanding of the sciences. Systematic attempts were also made to understand those human beings perceived as malfunctioning, whether in a medical sense, psychologically, or in terms of criminality.

Punishment and prison

During this period of reform there was a growing preoccupation with the idea of punishment as a means of reforming the offender, and also as a means of providing labour for the state. If punishment was to be economically effective, then it needed to reform offenders so that they would not re-offend, and be a cause of further cost to the state. There was also a desire to look for ways by which the prisoner could perform tasks which made an economic contribution towards the cost of their imprisonment.

Gradually the concept of the prison came to be viewed as the most effective means of judicial punishment. Foucault tried to produce a study 'not of the prison as an institution, but of the *practice of imprisonment*' (Faubion, *Michel Foucault: Power*, p. 225). Within its confines the state could impose a structure of discipline that would ensure a sense of control over the lives of those imprisoned. The discipline that they encountered within the prison would hopefully influence the lives of the prisoners once they were released. Society in the early nineteenth century was becoming more organized and structured, and the ordered life of the prison was a reflection of this external structure. This was also the period of the industrial revolution, and the mills and factories of this period also reflected this ideology of societal organization that was typical of the period. Prisoners and workers were likewise subjected to systems of strict control, enabling the state to use its power and authority to impose structure upon society.

Insight

Initially there was considerable resistance to the entire concept of prison as a means of punishment. Opponents of the idea preferred a form of punishment that seemed related to the original crime. However, prison proved to be an opportunity to try to reform, re-educate and retrain offenders, and as such it met the prevailing needs of society.

Foucault commented upon the work of Jeremy Bentham (1748–1832) who, in the late eighteenth century, designed a type of prison that reflected the prevailing ideology of scientific, structured observation. The essential idea was to create a prison design that would enable the maximum number of prisoners to be confined and monitored by the smallest number of observers. Bentham's architectural design was known as a Panopticon. The idealized structure of the Panopticon involved tiers of individual cells arranged in a circular pattern, with a central observation tower whose windows were opaque from the cells. Hence prisoners could not know when they were being observed and by how many prison officers. The intention was to create in the Panopticon a psychological atmosphere in which the prisoners felt under observation at all times. They had no idea how many officers were in the central tower, nor how many were in the prison at any one time. The Panopticon thus created internally the same type of atmosphere that the state intended to create in the external society – that of citizens being potentially observed at all times, and hence conforming to society's norms and values.

> ## Insight
>
> The exact design of the Panopticon was not used in very many actual prisons, although some of the basic ideas have found their way into many others. The idea of continual observation, and particularly observation where those observed have no idea whether or not they are being watched, has become an almost ubiquitous feature of contemporary society, both within large buildings and organizations, and as a feature of general urban life.

Foucault noted the extent to which the discipline associated with the prison was also extended by the state to the developing infrastructure of schools and hospitals. One of the essential characteristics of all these institutions was the application of methods of subdivision and categorization. Prisoners, for example, were placed in different categories, perhaps depending upon criteria such as their age or the nature of the offence committed. In other words, there was an increasing trend to document not only prisons and prisoners, but the remainder of society. In prisons, schools and hospitals the trend was the same, with a rapidly developing culture of record-keeping, described by Foucault as 'the integrated accountancy of individual records' (Gordon, *Michel Foucault: Power/Knowledge*, p. 71). The latter enabled considerable data to be kept on prisoners, and with that data evolved the possibility of studying prisoners as phenomena in their own right. The considerable quantity of data on the personal and occupational lives of prisoners enabled them to be studied as individuals, leading to the development of the new disciplines of psychology and psychiatry. For Foucault, however, this was not necessarily a virtue, but another facet of the developing ability of the state to exert administrative and bureaucratic control over its citizens.

Insight

We have now come to accept, although not necessarily to like, the extensive nature of the information that is maintained about individuals. The advent of computer databases has seen the phenomenon extend exponentially, until the citizen is nowadays rarely sure of the amount of personal information held by organizations and government agencies. Foucault saw this development as a feature of the control mechanisms of society.

Foucault also draws attention to the increasing culture of planning and organization in institutions. In prisons and in institutions for young people, the life of a prisoner was governed by a very rigid timetable. Times for eating, sleeping and work were precisely delineated. There was little scope for individual initiative. Prisoners became familiar with a regime of control under which all aspects of their lives were regulated.

Punishment, discipline and organization

For Foucault, there are several essential facets of this ideology of discipline that started to pervade society in the late eighteenth century and early nineteenth century. Perhaps the first element is the manner in which individuals are physically separated within institutions. Pupils in schools are placed in classrooms, patients in wards, and prison inmates are often in individual cells. As an element of this physical separation and confinement within a certain area, there is the process by which these physical divisions take place. Patients have to be separated into groups depending upon the nature of their illness and the extent to which cross-infection is possible. Pupils are divided into classes depending upon their ages and achievement levels; and prisoners are divided on varying bases including such factors as seriousness of the crime and length of sentence.

Insight

The idea of our being allocated a specific area within which we are permitted to sit or move is so prevalent in contemporary society that we tend to take it for granted. In schools, for example, pupils are allocated specific areas for learning, recreation and eating, and certain facilities and rooms may not be accessible to them. Life is thus strictly controlled, in much the same way as for individuals in other institutions.

It is also interesting, argued Foucault, that these institutions use a range of techniques to maintain discipline, and one of the most significant of these is hierarchical authority. Hospitals, schools, prisons and also factories operate very much on hierarchical principles. It is quite clear that such hierarchies operate among the staff. From the prison governor downwards through a hierarchy of prison officers, or from the nursing matron downwards through a range of nurses at different levels, a complete rank order of authority is evident. It is interesting, however, that discipline is also maintained through the extension of hierarchical authority to those who are confined. Thus in schools, there is often a complex hierarchy among the pupils of head boy or girl, prefects and form captains. In prisons also, some prisoners are given a range of responsibilities over their peers. The hierarchical system is thus all-pervasive, integrating discipline and control throughout the life of the institution.

The hierarchy, however, has a very important function, according to Foucault, in terms of the manner in which it maintains discipline. This function of hierarchy relates to the norms that constitute the accepted standards within the organization. The upper echelons of the hierarchy determine the norms that are to regulate the conduct of people within the organization. For example, in a school, the headteacher determines norms with regard to behaviour in the school, ranging from important issues such as bullying to less important matters such as whether pupils are permitted to walk on the grass. In a factory, the production manager may determine norms in relation to safety when operating machinery. In a hospital, the senior clinical manager may determine norms in relation to procedures for the issuing of drugs to patients. Norms establish yardsticks for behaviour that are functional in terms of supporting the hierarchy, and ensuring the coherence of the organization.

However, in order to form judgements about the adherence or otherwise to social norms, Foucault noted that organizational members had to be evaluated. Pupils, teachers, nurses, doctors and factory workers had to be assessed in relation to their capacity to comply with the accepted norms of the institution. Those who are successful in meeting the norms may find that they are moved up the hierarchy, while those who are unsuccessful are moved down. Nevertheless, it would seem that in the case of prisons such techniques are not particularly effective in terms of the long-term reduction in crime. Although designed to improve the conduct of offenders, it appears that prisons are not very effective in persuading offenders to move away from a life of crime.

In seeking to develop an explanation of criminality, the institution of the 'prison' and of the 'police' sought to try to explain certain elements in the cognitive and psychological makeup of individuals, and to link these features with certain types of criminal conduct. In other words, it started to become a possibility to consider a concept such as motivation, and to try to understand what a person was thinking immediately prior to committing a criminal act. If, for example, it was established that certain individuals were subject to feelings of aggression, the next logical step was to try to understand the cause of those feelings. The cause might, for example, be physiological, and in principle susceptible to being treated through clinical intervention. On the other hand, the cause might be located in the psychological consequences of the way in which the individual was brought up. In both of these hypothetical explanations there is the beginning of a radical departure in the understanding and treatment of criminality. In both cases, the individual is no longer 'blamed' for the acts committed, but rather the latter are explained through phenomena inherent in the person. The causes of the crime are in a sense removed from the deliberate will of the person, and explained in terms of either inheritance or social environment.

It is interesting to reflect upon the range of potential causes of the late eighteenth-century penal reforms. One might, for example, attribute the transition from a public and cruel execution to the disciplined, impersonal atmosphere of a modern prison, to a sense of moral outrage at conspicuous cruelty and torture. However, social change is invariably and inevitably complex, and it is usually almost impossible to specify with any accuracy the chain of causal events that lead from one social system to another. However, it is probably no accident that the penal reform movement coincided with the enormous economic changes of the industrial revolution. It has often been argued that the transformation of the educational system and the increased emphasis upon ensuring widespread numeracy and literacy was linked directly to the need to provide educated workers for the factories of the industrial revolution. If a country is to compete economically, then it needs an educated workforce to both design and develop technological innovation, and also to operate it once installed. This is an argument that governments have frequently made since the early nineteenth century.

In a sense the same arguments applied to prison reform. If society was to function as an integrated whole, then the prison system had to take in people who were dysfunctional and transform them into people who could leave prison and become effective contributors to the economic system. The result was that the prison system had to develop strategies for educating and for socializing prisoners into the norms and values of a working life. It was imperative for the economy of the country that inmates left prison with both the skills and motivation to contribute to the country's economy. These kind of sentiments undoubtedly pervaded the social and political planning of the period. We may not be able to point to a precise and linear causal connection, but there was undoubtedly a general sense that planning, structure and organization were required in society, if that society was to function efficiently in the modern world. Yet Foucault noted that 'prison indirectly produces delinquents' (Rabinow, *The Foucault Reader*, p. 229).

It is also perhaps interesting that, in the penal reforms, gradually much more attention was paid to crimes involving theft and other crimes against property and the possessions of people. This contrasted with the early eighteenth century when the crimes perceived as being the most serious were those that were a challenge in some way to the higher social classes of society. Ultimately, the most serious crime was one aimed at the monarchy. The late eighteenth century, however, saw the advent of a society that would become centrally preoccupied with material progress and with economic success. People were encouraged to work hard and to accumulate wealth. Any crime, therefore, that sought to misappropriate such wealth was regarded as very serious indeed, and the punishment commensurately severe.

It was, however, not generally possible to ensure the adherence of all citizens to a society based upon organization and discipline. People would forget their obligations or would not be able to sustain the required degree of attention needed to act according to the norms of the institution or society. One result of this was the advent of training. The purpose of training was not to educate people, or to render them capable of autonomous, critical thought. On the contrary, it was to make them capable of adhering automatically and without thinking to the defined norms of society. It was realized that training had an important place in prisons, schools and hospitals, quite apart of course from its traditional location in the armed forces or religious institutions. New systems of training were developed in order to make people more and more efficient in following accepted standards and values. With training came an ideology of testing and evaluation. It was necessary that those in authority had a clear idea of who had absorbed the required training and those who had not absorbed it. It was thus essential to test people in different contexts to ensure that they had internalized the required norms of behaviour. Eventually such testing became marked by the issuing of certificates and qualifications that validated the achievement of a specific standard in training.

Foucault stressed that one of the major ways in which society knows that its citizens are subscribing to the required norms is through an extensive system of observation. He noted in particular that one of the alleged strengths of the Panopticon was the fact that prisoners had no idea of whether or not they were being observed. They simply knew that the system had the power to observe them, that there was always the possibility that someone was in the central observation tower. This fact was therefore sufficient to persuade the inmates that it was advisable to adhere to expected behaviour patterns. There is a clear analogy with the modern system of video camera surveillance. We know the cameras exist; we can see them, yet are never absolutely certain how often or when we are being watched or filmed.

The role of the police is clearly related to that of observation, and yet it is interesting to reflect upon Foucault's analysis of the prime function of the police. Foucault relates this role very much to the economic importance of the individual in modern, capitalist society. The role of the police is clearly to maintain order, discipline and the adherence to norms in society, and yet the ultimate purpose of this is seen as reinforcing and supporting the function of the individual as contributing to the economy. The function of the police force is fundamentally to liberate the individual to contribute efficiently to society without the imposition of any unwelcome constraints that might restrict that contribution.

In *Discipline and Punish: The birth of the prison*, Foucault describes the regime in an orphanage and one can detect here the same ultimate purpose of discipline leading to a more functional role in society for the young people. He describes in particular the way in which the tiniest aspects of their lives were controlled by the establishment. The young people were expected to conform to the most detailed patterns of behaviour, and the slightest, most inconsequential infringement of this behaviour pattern was punished. Moreover, the punishments were almost as detailed and varied as the potential transgressions themselves. A multitude of different punishments could be selected in relation to a specific infringement. Young people thus became preoccupied with the need to adhere to the regulations.

The extent to which people are able to conform to the norms and regulations of organizations also came to be measured by examinations. The latter measured the competence and ability of people to meet formal requirements. Foucault notes how examinations began to assume a very formal character. It became normal in examinations for people to sit in rigid rows and to comply with a strict set of procedures during the examination. Failure to adhere to the procedures often resulted in automatic failure. The examination system also became a kind of metaphor for accepting the organizational system. It became a ritual in which acceptance of the examination system was an agreement to the legitimacy of the overall organization. It represented an acceptance of the inherent differences in power and authority, between those who imposed the examinations and those who took them. Foucault notes how the examination system was not a procedure simply added at the end of a period of schooling or of a training course. It was embedded within the education system, so that it became an inherent element. It was employed, along with teaching, as an essential element of the system of education and training. The examination system was immensely powerful in that it enabled those in authority to control large numbers of pupils or trainees. Those managing the system could decide on those young people who could declare themselves qualified; they could control financial rewards and promotions, and use the examination system to exert influence over careers.

Insight

We now tend to take for granted the idea of a society based upon certificated qualifications and competence. It is, however, an important system of social control, determining access to professions and the better remunerated jobs, and affording beneficial career development.

The regimes of schools, prisons, hospitals and other institutions all came to be supported by a very detailed system of record-keeping. In prisons, it became essential to document the progress of each prisoner. Those whose behaviour was acceptable, and who complied with the accepted norms, were recorded as suitable for potential early release or for some other form of reward. Yet Foucault was also sceptical, noting that 'detention causes recidivism' (Rabinow, *The Foucault Reader*, p. 226). The system could function only if every detail of the performance of each prisoner was recorded in detail. In hospitals it was also essential to document the progress of every patient, so that diseases could be studied and further infection prevented as far as possible. All organizations, certainly including the educational system, found it essential to maintain detailed records.

An important change that took place during this process was the increasing emphasis upon the individual as the object of study. It was no longer practical to think of human beings as members of groups, with general characteristics. Human beings needed to be considered as individuals, and separate records maintained of each one. In this process there was a great deal of attention paid to detail. No aspect of an individual's achievement or character was too small to be ignored in the record-keeping. Prisoners and school children alike had to pay attention to the smallest details of behaviour and submit to achievement testing, their results and performance noted in ever-lengthening records. This detailed record-keeping was also essential given the rapidly increasing population of Western Europe during the development of the industrial age. The larger number of people in all types of institutions, from factories to prisons, necessitated an extremely rigorous system of record-keeping.

There is a sense in which the prison system generates knowledge.
It does this by relating the different elements of society that combine
together to create a system of punishment. The legal and political
systems generate a system of codified laws that define the limits of
legal behaviour. Linked to this is the judicial system that determines
the guilt or innocence of people accused of crimes. The judicial
system also determines the level of punishment appropriate to a
particular infringement of the law. All of these aspects of knowledge
are integrated by the penal system into the knowledge that is
accumulated about the individual prisoner. It gradually became the
tendency to explore all aspects of the lives of prisoners, in order to
compile a study of the many factors that appeared to be integrated
with the commitment of the crime for which they were incarcerated.
There thus developed a kind of 'research' culture within which,
for example, possible explanations were created for the behaviour
patterns of convicted criminals.

10 THINGS TO REMEMBER

1   *Foucault contrasted two very different types of institutionalized punishment: that of the early eighteenth century with that of the modern era.*

2   *In the pre-modern era punishment was designed to demonstrate the power of the sovereign over the individual.*

3   *Such punishment, particularly for serious crime, often involved torture.*

4   *Punishment in the modern era was much less physical in nature, and more psychological.*

5   *Modern punishment was designed to control the individual and to emphasize the way in which the state was able to take over all aspects of a person's life.*

6   *For Foucault, an essential element of the modern system of punishment was observation of the individual.*

7   *Observation also included a system of detailed documentation of the individual citizen.*

8   *Foucault noted the Panopticon developed by Jeremy Bentham as an example of the attempt to control prisoners largely through a system of continuous observation.*

9   *In the modern era, according to Foucault, people in organizations were disciplined partly through a system of strict adherence to minor rules.*

10   *One of the functions of prison was to rehabilitate prisoners so that they could make a useful contribution to the economy.*

5

Living outside the norms

In this chapter you will learn about:
* *Foucault's analysis of the evolution of attitudes towards questions of sex*
* *his analysis of the medical and health model of discourse about sex*
* *Foucault's view of differences in attitudes towards sex between the West and the East.*

The history of attitudes towards sex

For most of his life Michel Foucault tended to explore experiences that were largely outside the norms of the majority of people. For example, on different occasions he experimented with hallucinatory drugs and also with sadomasochism. Clearly, he is not alone in seeking such experiences, although they remain outside the lifestyle of the mainstream of the population. The reasons for his seeking such experiences remain complex. One must assume that there was an element of personal predisposition, but there may well have been more complex motives. Foucault had undertaken a series of explorations of, for example, the history of sexuality, and had documented the way in which, in some historical eras, any public discussion of sex had been severely limited. It seems likely that he wished, at least partly, to explore the boundaries and limits to which one might take sexual and other experiences. He wanted, for example, to explore the ethics of participating in such experiences, and to examine the moral reasoning behind the exclusion of sexual discourse from the public domain. Foucault was interested in the subject of personal freedom vis-à-vis the desire of the state to limit such freedoms, and it appears that again he may have wished to explore such limits in practical rather than simply theoretical terms. However, whatever may have been the motives, these explorations constituted a distinctive element in Foucault's life.

Insight

For most of his life, Foucault was interested in the issue of personal freedom to explore whatever experiences the individual found interesting in order to develop and flourish as a person. Although he certainly would have accepted the right of the state to broadly control the nature of society, he nevertheless appeared to give pre-eminence to personal individuality in terms of exploring the world.

In his book *Histoire de la sexualité: Vol. 1, La Volonté de savoir* (1976; published in English as *History of Sexuality: Vol. 1* in 1978), Foucault documents some of the differences in the prevailing norms applied to the discussion of sexual matters in different historical periods. In addition, he also attempts to investigate some of the possible reasons for these changes in perception. In particular, he compares the situation in the early seventeenth century with that in Victorian times. Broadly speaking, he notes that in the former era sexual matters were freely discussed and treated as a normal part of human experience, whereas in the latter many social restrictions were placed on the open discussion of sex.

Foucault noted that during the Victorian period discussion of sexual matters, such as it existed, tended to take place, not in the general public domain, but only within the private confines of the home. Moreover, in that case also, discussion was seen as appropriate only between married couples.

In contrast to the situation in the seventeenth century, children, for example, were not expected to be aware of questions concerning sex and reproduction. The values and accepted standards for a discourse about sexual matters were defined by the orthodox, conventional married couple, and anything else was regarded as unacceptable. In seeking to understand and explain something of the reasons for the transition from a liberal society to one in which sex could not be openly discussed, Foucault looks first towards the burgeoning economic production of the industrial revolution. He hypothesizes that, within the industrial revolution, the prime ethic was one of continual and hard work, in order to maximize productivity. Within such an environment, there was little room for a philosophy of leisure or indulgence in pleasure. Certainly there was little scope for the idea that sexual activity could in any sense ever be regarded as recreational. Sexual activity had one purpose only within the ideology of the industrial revolution, and that was to reproduce humankind. Not only that, but the motivation for such reproduction was to create more workers to meet the requirements of industry. Any deviation from this purpose may have diluted the single-minded effort that was required to ensure a high level of productivity, and hence a high level of competitiveness for the state.

Insight

According to Foucault, the restrictions on discussions about sex had the consequence of placing serious limits upon the activities of people in the broad public sphere, and ensuring that they largely gave their attentions to productive work that contributed to the state's economic development.

Foucault also proposes a further, more complex argument to illuminate the nature of the discourse that seeks to liberate sexuality from a condition of repression. He starts his argument from a situation in which sexual discourse is repressed as in Victorian times, and links this repression to the exercise of power by those who would focus the attention of society on the needs of an industrial age. Foucault and those who would challenge a repressive ideology towards sexuality see advantages for society. They are promising the individual a transformation in society, and a vision of the future that will be more liberal and less constraining. Foucault is interested in the relationship between power and sex, and the interest shown by those in power in the way in which it might be useful to manipulate the discourse of sex. He is also interested in the notion that for a phenomenon that is simply a natural function, human beings appear very interested in controlling the way in which it is discussed, and the amount of time that can be devoted to considering it.

Insight

It seemed very interesting to Foucault that sexual activity was not treated by society as simply an 'activity'. It would be conceivable to think of sex as simply a biological activity similar to breathing, eating or digestion. However, that was not the case and Foucault was interested in the reason or reasons for this.

During the Victorian period, there were major changes in the manner in which sex was discussed. In some ways, it was still possible to discuss sex, but the vocabulary and the nature of the discourse had changed. Many of the more specific and precise words used to describe sexual matters were either deliberately suppressed or gradually disappeared from use. They were replaced by expressions that were either imprecise or were euphemisms, and which enabled a discourse to take place without the need to be explicit.

There were other trends in society, however, that had the effect of sustaining a discourse about sex. During the eighteenth century those who exerted political and economic power began to reflect upon those factors that encouraged industrial expansion and the resultant wealth creation, and also the variables that were affected by an expanding economy. Politicians and social planners began to be aware that there was a relationship between the state of the economy and human reproduction. In rather basic terms, if the economy was successful, and productivity was expanding, then people would have larger families. People would be wealthier and be able to feed and sustain larger families. Moreover, as those children came to maturity, they would be able to contribute to continuing economic success. In other words, it was in the interests of the state to consider the varying factors that had an influence upon population growth.

Once those in power started to reflect upon these questions, it was only a short step to realize that the state had a vested interest in the reproductive process. Sex was not simply a totally private matter, but something in which the state was interested. The sexual habits of people related directly to the birth rate, which was connected directly to matters of economic productivity. There was therefore a necessary and essential debate to be had about sexual habits, and this debate was of direct interest to the government. It is interesting, therefore, that the state was caught between two very different, and conflicting, types of discourse concerning sex. On the one hand, it was apparently useful for the government to suppress discussion about sex, as it enabled workers to concentrate on economic productivity; but, on the other hand, it was necessary for the government to sustain some type of discourse concerning sex because this was directly connected to debate about population expansion. Total suppression of anything connected with a discourse about sex would thus have been dysfunctional for society.

Foucault pointed out that although one might interpret the Victorian perspective on sexuality as one of repression, there are other possible hypotheses and interpretations. One of these is a perspective linked to the idea that the state is fundamentally concerned with the well-being of its citizens. In other words, sexual activity is controlled by the state because, if it were not, then some of the consequences could be harmful for people. These consequences might include greater numbers of illegitimate children, the spread of disease through sexual contact, and the breakup of marriages through extramarital relationships. There is also the possibility that some of these results could have had negative effects upon the capitalist system. Foucault was particularly interested in the way in which the state might be able to intervene to create a change in the type of discourse involving sexual matters.

The post-World War II period, and particularly the 1960s, saw the inception of a new paradigm with regard to sexual questions. The prevalent discourse of the period saw questions of sexuality merge with issues concerning politics, education, literature and the arts in general. The discourse on sexuality involved a largely laissez-faire approach, linked with openness in discussions about sexual matters. This liberal approach, however, was also linked to a left-wing political ideology, and centralist control by the state of economic planning. Throughout the 1960s and early 1970s the liberal social ideology was also very influential on the educational system. The prevalent view, which influenced a great deal of educational planning, was that there should be far less teacher-centred control over the curriculum, and indeed over pedagogy in general, and that much more emphasis should be placed upon the views of children and young people (see Chapter 3). The idea of asking children what they wanted to learn would have been anathema in a pre-war society, and yet now it became a very influential perspective. It was also a viewpoint that held considerable sway in terms of the design of new schools. The idea of the open-plan classroom, where children could move around freely and change their activities as they saw fit, was an example of this liberal educational philosophy. Moreover, there was considerable debate concerning the type of sex education that was desirable within such an educational system. There was a considerable weight of opinion that sex education should be more explicit, and should describe in greater detail the physical aspects of sex. Considerable attention was also given to guidance on contraception.

Insight

The overall trend from the late 1960s was towards providing more sex education for children and young people, though many teachers felt unsure how to approach this task. Some people felt that a clinical approach to sex education, without emotional education, might lead to greater promiscuity.

The overall atmosphere in the society of the period included such developments as more tolerant attitudes towards homosexuality, stronger demands for more gender equality, and wider experimentation in terms of types of marriage and in types of communal life. The new liberalism in sexuality was also encouraged by the availability of the contraceptive pill. It is also interesting that during this period sex became very closely linked with the capitalist system, through its capacity to assist in marketing and advertising. Sex became, arguably, the most potent means of helping to sell a product.

Differences between East and West

In general terms, one can discern a considerable hiatus between the philosophy of sexual activity in the East, and the approach in the Christian West. In the East, and one might cite the Kama Sutra in India as a prime example, there developed historically a perception of sexual activity as pleasure. It was an activity to be studied, to be learned, and was regarded as a positive element of life. Foucault contrasted this with the approach in the West, where the prevalent emotion associated with sex was one of guilt.

Insight

There was a great deal of interest in the 1960s and 1970s in 'Eastern' philosophies, especially those of India. The approach to learning and discovery about the self found in such philosophies was in harmony with the new generation in the West and their approach to sexuality.

In the West people were generally reluctant to discuss sexual experiences, as they were generally viewed as morally decadent and, even if they took place within the confines of marriage, as an inappropriate subject for general discussion. In India, however, love and sex were regarded not only as a suitable subject for discussion, but also as something in which to receive guidance from a guru or teacher. Knowledge about sex was passed on from teacher to pupil, much as one would transmit knowledge about anything else. The skills of sexual relations were studied, practised, written about, and taught. The situation in the West was quite the opposite. There was no sense in which sex was a suitable subject for teaching or transmission. There was no attempt to accumulate a body of knowledge about sexual activity. Quite the contrary. It was seen as something to exclude from general discussion.

Indeed, so linked was sex to a feelings of guilt that from medieval times onwards it was viewed by the church as a suitable topic for confession. People were expected to explain, under the conditions of the confessional, the activities in which they had been engaged and to seek the forgiveness of God. In extreme cases, during the medieval period, torture might even be used to encourage people to divulge information about their sexual activities. As we approach the modern period, such sentiments did not really change, although less harsh physical methods were adopted and replaced by a more psychological approach. The pressure of society was brought to bear upon people who appeared to behave in ways contrary to the conventions of society. In cases, for example, of extramarital infidelity, a community could exert great pressure on people to both confess their 'sins' and also to transform their behaviour. In some cases, they could be forced to leave the community, a considerable sanction in many cases, involving financial loss, and also perhaps the loss of employment.

Insight

As we have seen, Foucault asserted that the type of discourse associated with a particular historical period is a determining factor in the power relations of that period, including the prevalent norms. The discourse that combines a discussion of sex with that of guilt places the discussion within the remit of theology, and hence permits the church to both take a view on the issue and also to exert influence on it.

The medical model of sexuality

In the modern era there was one way in which discussion about sex became acceptable in the West, and that was through the adoption of a medical approach to sexual issues. By thinking about sex solely within the parameters of a medical model, it became possible to discuss almost any element of sexual activity. However, in order to achieve this, a process of definition had to take place: on the one hand, defining some aspects of sexual behaviour as 'healthy' and characteristic of a person who was in a sound state of medical equilibrium; and, on the other, defining other sorts of behaviour as symptomatic of an illness or sickness, and in need of treatment. This process of definition was not objective; rather it was a social construction, reflecting to some extent the norms and values of society, but more specifically mirroring those of the medical profession itself. Indeed, one might even argue that the need to subdivide sexual activity into two categories – the medically 'healthy', and the medically 'unwell' – was a social construction in itself. It would have been, for example, an intellectually tenable position simply to regard all sexual activity as a part of human behaviour, and not to subdivide it or categorize it. However, given the application by human beings of norms and values to most other areas of activity, it would perhaps have seemed unusual if this had not also happened with regard to sexual activity.

However, it was very easy within the framework of a medical model to use it to support the most conventional approaches to sex, and to define the remainder as clinical aberrations. It would be very easy, for example, to define homosexuality as a form of illness, and to support this by means of the full authority of the medical profession. The latter traditionally exercised a great deal of power, in particular through its capacity to define certain types of behaviour, physical condition or psychological state, as requiring treatment. Nevertheless, the medical model enabled discussions to take place about topics that otherwise would have been taboo, although it is a matter of debate whether an alternative framework for discussion of sex would have been more appropriate and functional for society.

In the modern era, as sex education found its way into the Western school curriculum, and came to be seen as desirable, a health or medical model was the predominant paradigm. Sessions were delivered often by a visiting nurse, who would describe the processes of sexual interaction, using clinical vocabulary and examples. The idea of 'pleasure' was rarely discussed, and nor was a great deal of attention given to the emotional dimension of the subject. If emotional aspects of sex were discussed, then normally this was done within the parameters of a traditional, heterosexual marriage. Eventually, however, it was realized that this approach resulted in giving children and young people a rather distorted, one-sided view of sexual relations, and that the emotional aspect of sex was arguably just as important as the physical. Gradually, there has been a change, so that today a more rounded, comprehensive approach is taken.

Insight

The medical discourse related to sex education tended to result in a formal, clinical discussion, which treated the subject almost as one might discuss a treatment for a medical condition. The advantage of this discourse is that it no doubt removes some of the embarrassment for the teacher. On the other hand, it provides the students with a rather limited and biased picture of the true nature of sexual relations.

It is part of Foucault's interest in studying sex to trace the way in which we speak of it, and the way in which it enters into our discourse. He is particularly interested in the way in which this has changed over the years. He notes that historians originally were concerned only with charting the key dates of history, the rules, the battles and the grand occasions. Eventually, it became clearer that it was possible to explore the social and economic history of societies. It was possible to trace the changes in the lives of ordinary people, and to examine the way in which changing economic circumstances affected their lives. Finally, and only relatively recently in the study of history, it is becoming clearer that it is possible to turn the focus of history, and the techniques of historical analysis, on the development of the human psyche and the way human beings react to the world around them, including the way in which they understand and speak of the experience of sex. This represents an enormous transition in the nature of history because it changes the focus to the way in which ideas are produced at different times in history, and the way in which ideas are expressed through discourse.

Foucault and homosexuality

Foucault had a particular interest in the manner in which society had treated homosexuals and responded to homosexuality. He notes that, in the late nineteenth century, there were early attempts to respond to the phenomenon of homosexuality. One of the earliest and crudest of responses was simply to imprison homosexuals. It was therefore defined as a crime requiring incarceration. On the other hand, there was also evident a medical paradigm, which saw homosexuality as an illness that required clinical intervention. Homosexuals thus required treatment to help them revert to the heterosexual norm of society. Sometimes homosexuals were perceived as licentious individuals who simply pursued pleasure wherever they could find it, and had no sense of responsibility in terms of behaving responsibly in society. On the other hand, some people saw them as similar to criminals. They were perceived as having committed illegal acts, and as requiring punishment of some kind.

Insight

In contemporary times there has been a very significant change in the type of discourse associated with homosexuality, including the adoption of such terms as 'stable same-sex relationship', and the use of the concept 'partner' instead of always speaking of 'man and wife'. These changes in discourse have had a considerable effect upon the public perceptions of homosexuality.

Foucault believed there was a tendency for society to be continually moved towards a uniformity, a middle ground, where those minorities who wished to be slightly different, or indeed were slightly different, were continually urged or pressurized to conform. One could argue that conformity appeals to those in power because a society of conformists is much easier to control. Such a society can be marshalled towards certain economic or military ends and citizens can more easily be persuaded to act in uniformity. Foucault, however, wanted to preserve the differences between people. This was evident in so many ways, but certainly in his reluctance to allow people to attach ideological labels to him. If he had allowed this, then he would have permitted his own membership of a particular intellectual group, and he did not want this. He wanted to be able to take whatever intellectual position he felt was necessary in relation to a particular issue or problem.

Foucault noted that this paternalistic trend in the control of society often masqueraded as government and authority caring for the welfare of the members of society. Government did not want its citizens to smoke, to overeat, to avoid taking exercise, to drink alcohol, to gamble, or to do any number of countless things that might conceivably have even the slightest deleterious effect upon health. And yet this obsession with reducing all the risks of life simply produces individuals with a type of paranoia. If we take this type of philosophy to the extreme, then we produce a society in which everyone tries to conform to some centrally defined criteria, and where people are as risk-averse as possible. Such a philosophy eliminates individuality and creativity.

Insight

State paternalism may perhaps reduce public expenditure to some extent on such things as health, but it will tend to produce a society where people will be reluctant to engage in any kind of risk, unless it is legally sanctioned. This may not be a functional society because from time to time many people may need to take risks, for example in setting up a new business or even saving another's life.

For Foucault, the tendency of those with power in society is to categorize groups that in many ways do not require categorization. For example he noted that throughout history, and in many different cultures, religions and societies, people of the same gender had been attracted to each other, and had established many variants of relationship. There had apparently not always been the need to attach a particular term to describe such people or their relationships. People, *all* people, possessed sexual attributes of various kinds, and simply used those attributes to either create pleasure for themselves or to reproduce. However, in the modern age, the concept homosexual had been developed to describe such relationships. Having created that category, other characteristics became attached to the category, so that homosexuals came to be perceived, and conceived of, in a certain manner. The concept of 'homosexual' was created and, having been created, it was then compared adversely with the category of 'heterosexual', which had been defined as the norm of society.

A related phenomenon that interested Foucault was that those who de facto belonged to the category 'homosexual', and who took pleasure and indeed pride in associating themselves with this category, were in a certain way supporting and justifying the type of categorization performed by those in authority. It is perhaps for this reason that, although Foucault was homosexual, he did not appear to try to attach himself to a group labelled as such. In other words, although he did not attempt to hide the fact that he was homosexual, neither to he seek to attach an identifying label to himself.

Foucault appears to have sought the motivation and inspiration for his academic work and writing in his own life experience. His experience of the world was thus the starting point, it would appear, for his explorations of the nature of ideas and their historical development. He also appears to have had a tendency to try to take his life experiences as far as he could possibly take them. However, he also understood, as an academic, that mere empirical experience is insufficient grounds on which to necessarily say anything valuable about the world. One person's experience does not make a theory. Nevertheless, he started with experience, and then tried to view the connections with the experiences of others, and also asked the difficult questions about the origins of such experiences, and the status of the knowledge that could be derived from them. This process perhaps explains why there is no precise and consistent methodological approach in his research. If he had taken a purely theoretical stance, then it would have been possible to create a theoretical edifice from the beginning. However, having used the starting point of experience, Foucault had to adapt his methodology to the specific needs of whatever he decided to investigate at the time. This perhaps explains partly why Foucault's writing often appears complex.

In the 1970s Foucault became fascinated by the culture of the United States, and in particular with that of California. It offered opportunities for both experimentation with drugs and also with further homosexual experiences. In 1975 he took LSD along with two American academics, although initially he was quite reluctant to try the drug. The American acquaintances persuaded Foucault that it would be a valuable experience, although Foucault was initially very doubtful. It is difficult to understand exactly the origins of that uncertainty and reluctance, but it was perhaps a fear of a loss of rationality and control over his intellectual powers. To take such a drug was to yield to something that would take over one's intellectual control, and perhaps for Foucault, as a trained rationalist all his life, this was an enormous barrier to overcome. At any rate it does appear that he found the experience both moving emotionally, and fulfilling intellectually, and he did not regret the experiment.

At the same time, the California of 1975, and San Francisco in particular, offered many opportunities for experiences among the growing gay community. San Francisco's 'alternative' cultures had begun to flourish in the late 1960s, and this development included a strong gay community. Foucault enjoyed the freedom and the sense of friendship within this community. An important question for Foucault, however, remained the issue of how one should state one's homosexuality within a wider societal framework, and in addition how one should relate to the growing politicization of homosexuality through the gay liberation movement. Foucault was perceived by the gay community as a sort of icon, and yet he appeared to resist attempts to persuade him to be a figurehead for the movement. He seemed to be particularly suspicious of the trend to make public declarations of one's homosexuality, as a kind of personal commitment to one particular sexual orientation. The justification behind his reluctance was his apparent dislike of attaching himself to one particular movement or ideology in relation to almost anything. He did not wish to be perceived as a 'homosexual', 'gay person', or activist for any gay liberation movement. He simply saw himself as a human being with certain sexual preferences.

....

Insight

In his reluctance to label himself or be labelled as a 'gay man', Foucault was being entirely consistent with his general approach to other ideologies or arguments. Just as he seemed to feel it was inappropriate to adopt a stance as an intellectual leader, he resisted the tendency of the gay liberation movement to adopt him as a figurehead.

....

Foucault was particularly interested in the sadomasochistic community of San Francisco, and visited a number of bars and clubs to participate in these activities. It is interesting to note, however, that in the homosexual 'S&M' community there was not the degree of violence or aggression that is perhaps popularly associated with this subculture. The culture of sadomasochism relies extensively upon the simulation of torture and violence, rather than its reality. Although a certain degree of pain may be generated by the activities, this is kept carefully under control. One of the main features of the community is therefore a high level of interpersonal trust. The simulations of sadomasochism can not operate safely unless the participants are able to completely trust each other and there is confidence that each partner understands the acceptable limits of the experience. In addition, it is essential that any participant has the freedom to disengage from the experience at any time. There needs to be no sense in which someone is trapped involuntarily within an experience or a simulated activity.

For Foucault, one of the pleasures of sadomasochism was the potential for allowing him to assume a different persona, and to step outside his normal existence. This harmonized very well with his conviction that virtually all of human existence was a social construction. In other words, we are what we are, because of the way in which we are conditioned by our upbringing, but also by the range of experiences in adulthood. Social construction also applied, according to Foucault, to our sexual desires. We are attracted to those people, those phenomena and those experiences to which society states we should be attracted.

By 1983 it was becoming evident, particularly among the gay community in California, that a previously unknown, serious, and very infectious illness was affecting people, and apparently, in particular, gay men. Foucault was aware of this, but appeared to treat it with a certain levity. He appeared to have no great fear of death, and preferred to continue his philosophy of experiencing life to the full, including sexual experiences. However, by the following year, Foucault had become ill, and he quickly reached the stage where he finally realized he was on the verge of death. Understandably, he appears to have gone through a process of re-evaluating his life.

In one area, however, Foucault had always remained adamant, and that was in his dislike for the idea of confessing. He seemed to have a profound distaste for the Christian practice of confession, whereby one thought about all of the many ways in which presumably one had failed to come up to some type of moral standard. He did not accept the notion that an external agency should impose moral standards upon the individual, who would then feel that he or she had failed in some way if they could not meet those exacting standards. He did not feel that the individual human being had any responsibility to unburden themselves in this way. For Foucault it was as if the act of confessing involved an attempt to reveal the internal truth about an individual, when such a truth did not in actual fact exist. The confessional approach to truth appeared to assume that for any individual it was in principle possible to articulate an objective picture of themselves, and the extent to which they had met the norms and standards externally imposed upon them. For Foucault however, adherence to external standards was not what human beings should be trying to achieve. Above all else, they should be trying to fulfil themselves. They should be reflecting upon what they have the potential to become, and then trying to achieve this.

There was, then, little purpose in asking what the truth was about someone; in asking how one could summarize a person in the most truthful way. For Foucault, this was an inappropriate question. In any case, Foucault considered that the truth about a person was not a fixed and determined entity. It was something that changed continuously, and hence was very difficult to specify. It was therefore an almost impossible task to set someone to say the truth about themselves. They might acquiesce to the request, but for Foucault it was doubtful whether the response could have any validity.

In any case, Foucault considered that, if a person did try to summarize themselves, and did try to tell the objective truth about their personality and the things they had done in their lives, then this very process subtracted something from them. In a sense it limited their future freedom to become what they wanted to become. It drew a barrier around their potential. In any case, the confession also assumes that one can define that which is wrong, that which is immoral. For Foucault, it was not constructive to talk about the immoral, or sin, or failure to meet ethical standards. One had to make of one's life what one could, and reflecting continually upon the alleged failings of the past was not a functional activity for a person.

However, Foucault also acknowledged that there was one sense in which he inevitably revealed himself. He reflected that, in the very act of writing, the intellectual must inevitably say something about himself or herself. It was not possible to be a writer, and simply to say something objective about the world, as if one could look down on the world from above in a dispassionate, and totally rational manner. The very act of writing involved the active participation of the writer. The latter needed to look at the world, and to interpret what was seen. That very act of interpretation involved the writer in a close interaction with that which was being analysed and discussed. To this degree, therefore, the writer did reveal himself to the world, and did attempt to tell the truth about himself. In the final analysis, this was a form of confession.

10 THINGS TO REMEMBER

1 *Foucault was interested in the ethics of people following their own instincts and interests in sexual matters, instead of trying to conform to socially defined norms.*

2 *He compared values and attitudes towards sex in the pre-Victorian period with those in modern and contemporary society; later in his life he wrote an account of sexuality among the Greeks and Romans.*

3 *In the Victorian period Foucault noted that discussion about sexual matters was seen only as appropriate within the context of marriage and within the home.*

4 *There may also have been a connection between the restrictions placed on discussion about sex and the industrialization of society: if workers were to be effective in the mills and factories, there was no time to be involved with leisure activities or to be over-concerned with sex.*

5 *In the 1960s and 1970s sex became much more integrated with an increasingly liberalized society, and also as part of a growing leisure culture.*

6 *The 'medical' model of sexuality defined sexual activity as something to be defined and analysed as physiological, metabolic, anatomical or psychological, and hence capable of being discussed in a forum where normally it could not be discussed.*

7 *In the East, and in India in particular, Foucault saw sex as being essentially about personal exploration and fulfilment; while in the West it was far more frequently perceived as a subject for religious confession.*

(Contd)

8 *Foucault was particularly interested in the way in which we have come to speak about sex, that is in the nature of discourse concerning sex.*

9 *He sought to analyse the nature of the concepts that were created by those in positions of power, and used to define certain types of sexual activity as either acceptable or outside the norms of society.*

10 *Foucault considered that a great deal of his writing was ultimately based on his personal experiences in life, and hence this empirical basis revealed a good deal about his own nature.*

6

···

The rational and the insane

In this chapter you will learn about:
- *Foucault's analysis of the history of insanity*
- *his view of how different societies perceived the insane*
- *his ideas about the way in which insanity is a social construction.*

_____

The social definition of insanity

In 1961 Foucault published a voluminous work entitled *Folie et déraison: histoire de la folie a l'âge classique*. When the book was later translated into English, it was given the title *Madness and Civilization*, a rather liberal translation of the more accurate 'Madness and Unreason'. Foucault's original title displays the focus of this work, which is in essence a history of how society has viewed insanity, or an absence of 'reason', in people.

The book, moreover, reflects a major interest of Foucault's that also emerges in other works – the nature of the institution in society. Foucault rejected the attempt to define him as a structuralist – that is, someone who places emphasis upon the way in which the lives of human beings are influenced by the power and structures of society. Nevertheless, he was very interested in the way in which society creates institutions to address the situation of individuals who are in some way different from the norm. Nowhere is this more significant than in the history of the way in which society treats the 'insane'. The latter word has been placed in inverted commas to emphasize the fact that definitions of insanity are problematic.

Insight

Foucault appeared to dislike the idea of being defined within the parameters of a specific philosophical, sociological, or historical 'school of thought'. He probably considered this to be too restricting, and that it would limit his ability to think freely about social and historical phenomena.

If we reflect upon our contemporary, postmodern understanding of the concept of insanity we can see that the concept embraces a number of different categories. We define, for example, individuals who have committed extremely violent acts against the person as 'insane' because we cannot envisage a 'sane' person acting in that way. We may not fully comprehend the causes of their acting in such a way, but the label 'insane' suffices to categorize them. It acts partly as a definitional mechanism, but also as a means of excluding them from the mainstream of society. The term provides a justification for placing them in an institution and separating them from the sane population. In the cases of those who have committed acts of extreme violence, it also of course serves as a mechanism for protecting society, and perhaps for protecting the individual defined as insane. Nevertheless, the use of the term may mask the social or psychological causes of the violence.

Insight

The term 'insane' may not effectively distinguish between those who are capable of being treated and rehabilitated in society, and those whom it will be difficult to treat and therefore may need to be separated from society. For example, an individual may have a tendency towards violent acts, but their violence may be defined in terms of a clinical abnormality, a metabolic imbalance, or a condition treatable by medication. In other words, the insanity is defined within the parameters of rationality. Foucault was interested in 'what authorities decided about their madness' (Rabinow, *Michel Foucault: Ethics*, p. 5).

One of Foucault's major contributions to the study of insanity was to point to the process of social definition that exists in our view of the insane. In other words, insanity does not exist as a concept in its own right, but is a social production, depending upon the attitudes of society at a particular moment in history. This concept of insanity held at a specific historical period will have important consequences for the way the 'insane' are treated.

Insight

One difficulty with Foucault's understanding of 'insanity', sometimes referred to as the 'sociology of knowledge perspective', is that it can lead to a form of relativism. In other words, when we view knowledge as merely constructed by society, then there ceases to be a precise definition of insanity, leaving only a range of definitions depending upon the perception of society at that time.

In contemporary society there are many characteristics of behaviour or of psychological condition that may place someone outside the parameters of 'normal', 'sane' society. These characteristics or types may include unusual behaviour, social recluses, depression, communication difficulties, and social adjustment difficulties. In some cases, individuals may not be able to challenge the social definition of insanity, either through not having a support network of friends or relatives, or not being able to articulate clearly their own views of their condition. Even in modern times young people have been unable to resist their institutionalization as insane, and have then spent many years in institutions, without the social process being challenged.

Central to Foucault's concept of insanity is that the characteristics associated with the insane should not always be perceived as negative. Some may have insights into society and the way it functions, which, while being unorthodox, may nevertheless shed light on its inadequacies. Society, however, does not always wish its inadequacies to be revealed, and may prefer to define those who make such observations as being outside the parameters of sanity. From this perspective one might argue that many people in society perceive society as 'normal', when in fact there is much unfairness or many irrationalities inherent in it. Those who we define as 'insane' may notice some of these irrational aspects, but their views may not be accepted by the majority.

The history of interpreting insanity

In *Madness and Civilization* Foucault presents us with a history of the changing social definition of insanity from the Middle Ages to the nineteenth century. As Foucault has argued, the history of this process has not necessarily been one of evolution from inadequate ideas to enlightened ones. Indeed, as Foucault pointed out, the view of insanity as demonstrating something dangerous and potentially destructive of society, is a relatively recent phenomenon. In the Middle Ages, according to Foucault, it was leprosy, rather than insanity, that was seen as a threat to the stability of society. In fact, societies have always been concerned with stability, and with those aspects that might undermine that stability. Although societies have generally seen the need to respond to external changes or threats, their greatest preoccupation has been with the measures needed to sustain stability. Leprosy was a challenge to stability in the Middle Ages because of its accompanying physical deformities and because of the apparently random manner in which it afflicted people. It could easily be perceived as a divine punishment for wrongs committed in this earthly life. Hence lepers were often perceived as beyond civilized society, and indeed were placed in leper houses, well outside the walls of cities. The insane, on the other hand, were not perceived as a threat to society in the same way. They were rather seen as representing an alternative view of the world, but not one that was necessarily a challenge to society. They might be seen alternately as strange, amusing, eccentric, or the object of derision, but less as a threat to social stability.

The combined effects of the separation and confinement of lepers, and improved social conditions, led to a reduction in leprosy by the Renaissance period. Leprosy no longer appeared, according to Foucault, as the threat it had previously been, and insanity now assumed a greater significance in society. There appeared to be a need to deal with insanity in a more systematic manner. During the Renaissance period, there began to be systematic attempts to exclude the insane from towns and cities. A variety of methods were employed such as placing them in the care of religious communities or simply expelling them so that they were condemned to a life of wandering. These were the first signs of a systematic definition of the insane as unacceptable within society.

This tendency continued, as Foucault argued, into the classical age, so that, by about the mid-seventeenth century, there was a developing strategy to confine the insane in institutions. The insane had begun to be perceived as a potential threat to the stability of society. This process of social definition was also applied, however, to other sections of society, notably the extremely poor, the homeless, the ill and the unemployed. In other words, there was a reclassification of those social groups as deviant. Anyone coming within this category of deviance was subject to confinement and incarceration, primarily because they were seen as a potential challenge to society. The insane were thus grouped with many other types of social outcast, and systematically confined. There was, moreover, an additional, economic purpose to this policy. As the nature and success of the economy fluctuated, those in confinement could be drawn upon as a source of cheap labour for unskilled but necessary work.

The large-scale confinement of people of many different categories was not, however, a panacea for the ills of society. Poverty still existed throughout seventeenth-century Europe, and the confinement of some of the poor did nothing to eliminate it, although it may have masked it to some small extent. Equally, it was one thing to remove large numbers of the poor, unemployed and social misfits from society, but it was quite another to decide on how they should be managed and dealt with in the houses of confinement. Although they could be given some work within confinement, they might also at times be required in the external society depending upon the needs of the economy.

Gradually, throughout the seventeenth and eighteenth centuries, as Foucault indicated, there was a growing realization that it was not necessarily an ideal policy to confine large numbers of those who might be termed the 'socially undesirable'. By the end of the eighteenth century there appears a gradual transition in policy, and there is less of a tendency to confine the poor and destitute. From this period onwards there was a gradual realization that mass labour was necessary for the future of society, and hence that all those who could do some form of productive work were required to contribute in some way. Only the insane were to some extent perceived as unable to contribute, and hence were placed in confinement.

By the beginning of the nineteenth century, the social category attracting most attention in terms of a need to confine them, were the insane. In addition, there were the beginnings of a systematic attempt to analyse the nature of insanity and to treat it. In short, the notion of the insane asylum makes its appearance. With it also comes the definition of insanity as 'illness', and indeed something that can be studied and treated.

Insight

One result of the rise of science and rationality in the nineteenth century was that any world view opposed to the rational, for example insanity, was addressed through the medium of science. The methods of science, of attempting to understand cognitive processes, were brought to bear on the study of insanity.

During the period of large-scale confinement, some doctors were attached to the institutions, but they were generally there to treat medical conditions, rather than specifically to analyse the needs of the insane. However, with the advent of specialist asylums, Foucault argues, a change took place in the perception of insanity. Rather than being seen – as they were in the Middle Ages, or indeed in the classical period – as possessing a tangible world view despite their deviating from the norm, they were now perceived as medically or cognitively deficient and requiring remedial treatment. Previously any attempt at understanding the nature of insanity had seen it as a combination of physical and mental imperfections. Now, however, with the development of the asylum in the nineteenth century, there evolved an analysis of insanity that was more specifically cognitive. This prepared the way for the evolution of psychiatry as a specific subject area and indeed for its development as a science.

Foucault is, in a sense, as critical of the nineteenth-century regime as he is of the eighteenth-century treatment of the insane. He argues that a policy of physical restraint had been replaced by a policy that, though perhaps less physically inclined, was equally oppressive. The guardians of the insane, and also the doctors, did not seek to communicate with their wards. The insane did not have the opportunity to express anything of their own feelings, ideas or emotions. Even if they possessed the capacity from time to time, they were not permitted to engage in reflective discussion concerning their condition. Moreover, they were continually observed in their every action, and this observation exerted a form of oppressive restraint upon them.

Foucault also notes that one of the key functions of the doctors in the insane asylums was to define the characteristics of those who should be admitted. More than that, the doctors also issued the documentation which accompanied admission. Thus the early stages of the development of psychiatry were accompanied by the elements of a clinical bureaucracy. Insanity was gradually becoming a condition with definable characteristics, which could be certificated by doctors, and which could hence be treated. This development could be seen as a manifestation of the tendency towards bureaucracy in society. As society became gradually more regulated, then documentation and record-keeping increased in parallel. As Foucault pointed out, this was in itself a form of power and authority, as people needed to comply with the requirements of the medical diagnosis.

Once defined as insane, individuals had little choice over being admitted and treated. They had to submit to a clinical-bureaucratic regime, supported by the state. Although some might have regarded this as a more benign system than that of the classical period, for Foucault it was an equal, if not more subtle, means of repression and social control.

The advent of psychiatry

During the nineteenth century it began to be the case that individuals could claim that someone should be admitted to an asylum and ask that their mental state be considered by a psychiatrist. In such cases, the criterion was often that of whether the person was potentially dangerous within society. The classification of people into those who were, and those who were not, potentially dangerous to others, was often a difficult, if not impossible, task. Yet this became an increasingly significant feature of the psychiatrist's role.

Foucault was ambivalent about the modern science of psychiatry, which, although appearing to be benign and caring of the insane, appeared to him in some ways as oppressive as earlier regimes. It may not have been as physically cruel, but appeared as controlling through other measures. The contribution of Foucault to this debate was that he saw the insane as human beings, who, although in possession of a different perception of the world, and albeit with a lack of rationality, were nonetheless human.

10 THINGS TO REMEMBER

1 *In 1961 Foucault published* Folie et déraison: histoire de la folie à l'âge classique, *literally translated as 'Madness and unreason: a history of madness in the classical age'.*

2 *Foucault was interested in the nature of institutions and how they controlled people.*

3 *He examined the issue of the way societies deal with people who are in some way different from the norm.*

4 *Foucault perceived insanity as in some ways a 'social construction'.*

5 *He considered that insanity tends not to have an absolute identity of its own, but is defined as a society wishes to define it.*

6 *He perceived insanity, not as a single characteristic, but as a complex range of cognitive reactions and responses.*

7 *For Foucault, insanity was not necessarily a negative characteristic, as the insane were sometimes in his view capable of illuminating insights into society.*

8 *Foucault traced the historical development of changing views of insanity.*

9 *By the beginning of the nineteenth century Foucault noted the systematic attempts to confine the insane and to study insanity scientifically.*

10 *Foucault considered that the modern science of psychiatry, although presenting itself as a caring profession, was in some respects as oppressive as the procedures associated with earlier historical periods.*

7

Political engagement

In this chapter you will learn about:
- *Foucault's approach to political issues and the assistance he gave to human rights organizations*
- *his involvement in the events of May 1968 in Paris*
- *his engagement with the politics of educational change.*

Involvement in party politics

One of the key themes with which Michel Foucault was concerned throughout his life was that of power. In particular, he was interested in the way in which those in power were able to define the nature of the discourse about a certain subject, and hence control, to some extent, the concepts and ideas that were used. Power enables people and organizations to define the way that we look at the world, and if necessary to define the world in a way that is economically or politically advantageous to them. Those who do not possess power and authority may find that they are defined in a less advantageous manner, and hence their relatively lowly status may be reinforced. They may not have the opportunity to raise their economic status, or to become politically influential.

Particularly in his later life Foucault supported a range of social causes, adding weight to the claims of groups who had relatively little influence or power. Perhaps the first sign of this tendency to support the less powerful was when he joined the French Communist Party in 1950. He was apparently influenced in this by a philosophy lecturer at the Ecole normale supérieure, Louis Althusser. While having some sympathy with the Marxist ideology of the party, Foucault found other aspects of being a Party member rather difficult. In fact, as Foucault noted, 'the turnover of young people passing through the Communist Party was very rapid' (Faubion, *Michel Foucault: Power*, p. 249). Principal among his problems was that, as with most political parties, Foucault was expected to reflect the views of the Party in everything. He no doubt felt that he was in danger of abandoning his intellectual independence in the interests of supporting the Party, and he found this very difficult to accept.

Insight

Many academics do in fact work and write from a particular theoretical viewpoint. This might be for example, from the left or right of the political spectrum, and this may in turn affect their view of, say, economic issues. Nevertheless, one might argue that trying to remain independent of theoretical perspectives is also, in a way, a type of ideological position. It could be argued that everyone inevitably adopts a theoretical orientation, derived from many sources, including their education, upbringing and cultural background.

As we have seen throughout this book, there is ample evidence that Foucault valued, almost above all else, his freedom of thought and capacity to say whatever he wished in response to the issues of the day. He particularly objected to the types of Soviet propaganda prevalent at the time, and to the persecution of groups of people within the Soviet Union. He found it difficult to accept the way in which the French Communist Party appeared to accept and support the actions and justifications provided by the Soviets. Hence in 1953 he seems to have finally resigned from the Communist Party, after a membership period of only about three years. During the period until the late 1960s Foucault tended to concentrate on his academic career, writing books and gradually enhancing his reputation as a leading intellectual. It was the events of May 1968 that brought him truly into the public consciousness in France and subsequently across the world.

The politics of revolt

The events of May 1968 in Paris, took place against a broader backdrop across the world, which in essence involved a clash of world views between a younger generation opposed to capitalism, materialism and broadly right-wing politics, and the established generation that supported a liberal economic policy and traditional values, whether in terms of the family, the education system or government. Many circumstances contributed to the situation that erupted in May 1968, and it is not easy to identify a particular sequence of events. However, it was in the fields of employment and, in particular, education that a good deal of the conflict took place.

The Nanterre campus of the University of Paris was an early focus of dissent. In March 1968 a group of students met there to discuss the financing of the university and also the social class system in France. The students outstayed their welcome and the university administration called out the police. The smouldering conflict between students, lecturers and the university management continued over the coming weeks, until in early May the university authorities decided to close the university. There was an immediate reaction from the staff and students at the Sorbonne, in the centre of Paris. They protested against the closure of Nanterre and police moved in to occupy many of the Sorbonne buildings. Things came to a head on 10 May when students started to erect barricades and to dig up and throw paving stones at the police. There were numerous injuries among both the police and the demonstrators. Three days later there was a spontaneous general strike throughout France.

The situation became even more intense throughout the remainder of May. More and more workers went on strike – at the height of the action, approximately 11 million workers refused to work. Some workers attempted to take control of their factories and to run them in place of the management. There were further marches in Paris and the government of General de Gaulle was clearly on the verge of collapse. The President, however, managed to hold on to power. He stated that there would be a general election in June and ordered workers to resume work in the factories. There appeared to be an underlying threat that he would use the army to restore order in the country, if they did not. The disruption did start to diminish – it was as if the demonstrators had grown tired of the unrest. Workers returned to the factories and the students left their 'sit-ins' at the universities. Apart from a slight resurgence of protest in July, the events of May 1968 appeared to have ended. However, the government in France had been shocked into action, and there were numerous reforms, particularly in the education system.

During the previous two years Foucault had been living and working in Tunisia. He had taught at the University of Tunis and continued with his writing. Nevertheless, despite the quiet life that he led, he had remained interested in the developments in Paris, and people had phoned him to ensure he kept up to date with events. Eventually, towards the end of May he decided that he had to witness what was going on for himself and he went to Paris. From a philosophical point of view, he was very interested in the purposes and ultimate aims of the protests. It seemed to him that the students in particular, quite apart from the reforms that they sought in society, wished for a new human consciousness that would take humanity towards the twenty-first century.

There was a clear sense in Paris in May 1968 that the students and young workers wanted to confront the establishment and to overturn the status quo, using, in Foucault's words, 'a theory that was derived more or less directly from Marxism' (Rabinow, *Michel Foucault: Ethics*, p. 115). They wanted to challenge those who were in power, and to redistribute that power, so that a new world could be created – more liberal, more egalitarian, and with a different sense of ethics. The 1960s was not a decade free of war and conflict around the world, notably in Vietnam, and the demonstrators also wanted a world in which people lived together in greater peace and freedom. The students' aims were somewhat utopian and vague, and it was not always easy to see how these different ends could actually be achieved.

The events of May 1968 may have appeared to be a failure from
the point of view of the young people taking part, in the sense that,
on the surface at least, the political and governmental status quo
continued and life appeared to carry on much as before. However,
the government and political elite of France had been shaken,
and at one point must have at least considered it a possibility that
the government would be overthrown by a popular revolution.
It was almost certainly the psychological shock of this that jolted
the government into a range of reforms, particularly in the sphere
of education. Edgar Faure was appointed to the post of Minister
for National Education in the government of Maurice Couve de
Murville. The position of Edgar Faure was an extremely complex
one, but he set about developing changes in both the school system
and in universities. In terms of schools, there was a distinct shift of
emphasis within the overall philosophy of the school system. Pupils
and students were consulted far more about the nature of the
education they were to receive. The traditional didactic system of
French education was transformed into a much more participative
system. Teachers were encouraged to become more the facilitators
and organizers of an educational experience, rather than the
transmitters of knowledge.

disciplines, was being challenged by more 'student-centred' methods. Within this perspective, the curriculum was driven less by convention, and more by the developing interests of children and students.

It was, however, in the sphere of higher education that the greatest changes were apparent, and these changes became enshrined in the so-called 'loi Faure' passed in November 1968. This law reformed both the administration of universities and also the curriculum. In general terms, it increased the individual power and autonomy of universities. In terms of the management of universities, the law made provision for students, technicians and administrators to be members of university senates. In addition, universities were encouraged to ensure that they included employer and trade union representatives on their key committees. In terms of the curriculum, universities were also encouraged to combine traditional subjects to form new courses that were more relevant to the contemporary world. Finally, there was a tendency to merge the teacher and researcher roles, so that both could gain something from each other.

Insight

European universities had always been relatively elitist. They admitted only a relatively small proportion of the relevant age group, and competition for places was hence quite intense. The changes ushered in after the conflict of 1968 were the precursors of a mass higher education system that began to open up universities to social groups that in the past would have had no access to them.

The events at Vincennes

One of the most celebrated outcomes of the reforms, however, was the creation of the Experimental University Centre of Vincennes. This was created on the basis of a similar philosophy to that described above in relation to the schools sector. There was intended to be a sense in which lecturers and students worked collaboratively, rather than one simply transmitting knowledge to the other. It was intended to be an institution that created a new tradition, in opposition to the accepted academic model of a university. It was to be a university that established close links with the surrounding community and the organizations in the vicinity. It was also intended to encourage the enrolment of overseas students. Foucault was invited to become the head of the new Philosophy Department at Vincennes, and he readily accepted. He was not the only innovative academic to work there. At various times Gilles Deleuze (1925–95), Jean-François Lyotard (1924–98) and Jacques Lacan (1901–81) taught there. The subjects and courses available at Vincennes were very non-traditional for the French university sector at the time, and included theatre and cinema studies as well as psychoanalysis.

Insight

The history of university education throughout the world, has been one of the diversification of subjects taught and researched. In the medieval world, universities were often devoted to the study of theology and philosophy. Other subjects such as Classical languages and medicine were added later. The real expansion in the subjects studied came in the twentieth century, however, and it interesting to examine the late appearance of subjects such as engineering.

The university at Vincennes also welcomed adult students and provided classes in the evenings so that those who were in employment could attend and further their qualifications. However, one of the most interesting aspects of Vincennes, and the one with which people generally associate it, is the fact that it became such a political campus. By its very nature, it tended to attract left-wing activists who had scant respect for the educational establishment. Their view of education was that it had become part of contemporary capitalism and was now a commodity to be purchased in the same way as other goods or services. They believed that, instead, education should be available to all those who wanted it, and that it should be free. For this reason, many such activists viewed Vincennes not as an experimental university that set out to be radically different to the established institutions, but rather as a thinly disguised attempt by the existing political powers to defuse remaining elements of the rebellion of 1968.

All the same, there developed at Vincennes a particular approach to teaching that was fundamentally different to that which had existed previously in French universities. It was argued that teaching should certainly not involve the passive transmission of accepted knowledge about a subject. Rather it should involve an education in how to challenge the existing social order. There was therefore no real attempt made to teach the classic approaches to philosophy or to sociology, except in so far as they were useful in exposing the alleged inadequacies of the contemporary social and political system in France. Certainly, it was the prevalent view at Vincennes that a university education system should not be too dependent upon the lecturers, and that too much power and authority should not be vested in them. It was generally felt that the relationship between students and lecturers should be more equal and mutually supportive.

Another significant feature of the teaching style at Vincennes was the way in which curricular material was presented. It is traditional in education, at whatever level, to provide a structure or scheme of work that sets a particular topic in relation to other connected subjects. A scheme of work or curriculum is also very often sequential in nature. In other words, one starts with the 'easy' material and progresses to the more complex concepts. So engrained in us is this system that we rarely challenge its logic. Yet that is exactly what the lecturers at Vincennes chose to do. They delivered subject material in any order, or no order, leaving students to make 'connections'. The argument of the lecturers was that traditional sequences of knowledge or subjects simply reflected a traditional view of knowledge, with all kinds of inherent assumptions. They preferred to reject this completely, and to change totally the ideology of their teaching. One of the problems with the traditional approach to university teaching, according to Foucault and his colleagues, was that it placed the students in a position of dependency. The students had continually to appeal to the lecturers to explain how one writer related to another, or how one theoretical school of ideas related to another school.

Yet with the approach of the staff at Vincennes, the students were encouraged to do this for themselves. One of the results of this approach was that students had to read material in a much more active way. They had to carry out their own interpretive work.

Insight

Educationally the Vincennes ethos might be considered rather high risk. Students could have been left entirely floundering, with no real understanding of their subject material. On the other hand, it did create independent learners, and the general approach is quite familiar to many lecturers today, who encourage students to develop their own learning strategies.

This approach may perhaps have left some students feeling a little uncertain and undirected in their studies, but it at least encouraged them to be much more active in their reading, and much less reliant on the authoritative judgements of the academic staff. One might argue, as did many of the academic staff at Vincennes, that good teaching should not involve lecturers merely transmitting the subject matter with which they feel familiar. Quite the contrary. Good teaching should involve research; it should involve an investigation of something; it should involve examining issues with which both lecturers and students are unfamiliar. This leads, according to the Vincennes philosophy, to a truer sense of what education should really be about.

In planning the operation at Vincennes, Foucault and his colleagues attempted to put in place, not only these new teaching methods, but also a breadth of subject matter that had not previously been evident in the French university system. Nevertheless, these measures did not satisfy all the different left-wing student groups existing at Vincennes. For many of them, this experimental university centre remained merely a reflection of the status quo in France. In January 1969 students took over the main building at Vincennes, prompting a police attempt to regain control. A number of staff, including Foucault, sided with the students and took part in actions such as the throwing of stones and other missiles at the police. Foucault's involvement in the practical matter of rebellion gave him a growing reputation as a militant. However, he appears to have been slightly disenchanted with the way in which this revolutionary activity caused him to take time away from his writing. The following year he was able to leave Vincennes and take up a professorship at arguably France's leading intellectual institution, the Collège de France.

The Collège de France was founded in 1515 by François I, initially as an institution for the study and teaching of subjects such as mathematics that were not then taught at the University of Paris. It has since evolved to become a very distinctive institution, with, at the present time, fifty-two professors, working in a wide range of subjects. New professors are elected solely by the existing post holders. It is interesting that the Collège does not award any qualifications at all, nor does it engage in any form of assessment. The professors are all engaged in research and writing, and at regular intervals they give lectures on their research. Any member of the public can attend their lectures. This was a very prestigious post for Foucault and the status of being a professor at the Collège enabled him to exert considerable influence.

Politics and social reform

Foucault's long-term partner, Daniel Defert, who lectured in sociology at Vincennes, had some considerable influence on him in terms of his involvement in political action. Defert, for example, was a member of the Gauche prolétarienne, an extreme left-wing organization that had been created in 1968, partly as a result of the student protests. The government regarded it as an unacceptably extreme organization, and several years later it was proscribed. It never had many members, but because of the radical nature of its policies, it tended to exert considerable influence on left-wing policies and thinking. It specifically tried to place its young intellectuals to work in factories, where they would be able to influence the thinking of the unions and other workers' organizations. Even after the organization was officially banned, it continued to operate in secret.

It was several months after Foucault had obtained his chair at the Collège de France that he reflected upon the possibility of starting a pressure group on prison reform. His own academic research into the history of confinement had given him a strong interest in the subject, and he felt that the conditions in many French prisons were unacceptable. He founded the Groupe d'information sur les prisons (Information group on prisons; GIP), an organization that attracted the support of Defert and his friends in the Gauche prolétarienne, especially as they had left-wing colleagues who were in prison. The purpose of the GIP was initially to gather empirical evidence from people who had been in prison, and also from visits to prisons, in order to document the prevailing conditions. Foucault's approach was in keeping with his general philosophy of the nature of the intellectual. That was that it was not the purpose of intellectuals to proclaim exactly how the government should act in certain circumstances, or exactly what should be the conditions in prisons, but rather to expose in as much detail as possible the conditions under which prisoners existed. Other forces in society, armed with this evidence, could then proceed to bring pressure for change.

Insight

Foucault adhered consistently to a philosophical position in which he used his skills as an academic to collect and disseminate data, but avoided, wherever possible, becoming involved as a political activist. The dividing line between these roles is sometimes not very clear, but with Foucault the existence of this division of roles became something of a matter of principle.

The GIP seems to have had an extremely informal structure. This was in a sense compatible with Foucault's view of organizations. He had always been opposed to the way in which the organization and hierarchies of institutions were used as a medium for the exercise of power. With his own organization, it is consistent that he should not wish to set himself at the head of a hierarchy that made statements about policy and the way in which the organization should be administered. This perspective was to some extent at the heart of the differences between Sartre and Foucault. Foucault felt that Sartre was in effect intellectually condescending in advising people on the appropriate ideological stance to take in response to issues. Foucault felt this was inappropriate, and that the role of the intellectual should simply be to present evidence and to leave individuals to formulate their own views.

Foucault and his colleagues employed questionnaires to try to collect systematic data from the prisons. They would wait outside prisons at visiting times and explain what they were trying to achieve to the families of prisoners. Foucault also invited ex-prisoners and their families to his apartment, in order to discuss prison conditions.

One of Foucault's key arguments and, indeed, political strategies was to try to encourage different agencies involved with prisoners and prisons to collaborate rather than to work independently. For example, he argued that doctors, welfare workers, prison officers, psychiatrists, social workers and the various officers of the legal system had a tendency to simply carry out their own individual job according to the criteria of their profession. This often meant that there were significant gaps between their roles and responsibilities and these resulted in adverse provision and care for prisoners. It was not that there were deliberate omissions in what the different agencies were trying to achieve, but simply that the overall effect was a service of diminished quality for prisoners. Foucault tried to encourage these agencies to work together effectively in order to provide a coherent service. Foucault continued his work on behalf of prisoners through the early 1970s. It would have been exhausting work, involving participation in demonstrations, the writing of pamphlets for distribution, giving talks, and generally trying to marshal support for the cause. There must also have been considerable psychological pressure upon Foucault, as his work brought him into direct confrontation with the police and legal authorities.

It is perhaps only natural that different pressure groups and radical political groupings began to seek Foucault's help and support. These groups represented a variety of different political causes, all broadly of a left-wing nature. Foucault was becoming a high-profile figure, whose sponsorship of a cause could attract useful media attention. In addition, Foucault was a dynamic public speaker, who could act as an influential advocate for causes. To differing degrees, Foucault supported groups campaigning against, for instance, the American involvement in Vietnam, against alleged police violence and mistreatment of people at demonstrations, and against the treatment of patients in psychiatric hospitals.

Insight

The fact that Foucault held a chair at the Collège de France gave him enormous cachet. As a member of one of the country's most prestigious academic establishments, he and his opinions would be taken seriously even by those who might otherwise simply regard him as a supporter of left-wing causes.

Foucault was no doubt aware of the possibility that he could easily be viewed as an archetypal left-wing, intellectual activist who supported all the traditional left-wing causes. There were two implicit difficulties here for Foucault. The first was that, by supporting such a wide range of causes, he would perhaps lose a certain degree of conviction when he did speak out against something in which he believed profoundly. People might be less likely to be convinced about the genuine nature of his feelings. The other issue was that he was in danger of becoming the very kind of liberal intellectual that he had criticized, most pertinently with regard to Sartre. To some extent he had argued that Sartre had lost the very kind of credibility that he was now in danger of losing himself.

The early 1970s also saw the establishment of a gay pressure group, the Front homosexual d'action revolutionnaire (Front for revolutionary action on homosexuality; FHAR). Foucault was interested in this movement, but did not, however, take a really active role. He was clearly ambivalent about the use of the word 'gay' and was unsure about the long-term consequences of adopting such a label. There may, however, have been a deeper philosophical basis to Foucault's apparent reluctance to become too involved in gay rights activism. He always seems to have had an antipathy to becoming labelled as a particular type of activist. It may be that his reluctance was based in a fundamental opposition to being defined in a particular way. He appears to have preferred to simply 'be' gay, rather than spend a great deal of time talking about it and discussing it. Nevertheless, he was deeply committed to the idea of equality for the gay community and felt very strongly about any exercise of power to limit that equality.

By 1975 Foucault was continuing to be politically active, representing a number of different causes. In that year, a particular cause célèbre among left-wing groups in Europe was the proposed execution of ten opponents of the right-wing government of General Franco in Spain. Of the ten people sentenced to death, two were members of the Basque Homeland and Freedom organization, or ETA. Socialists in France were particularly incensed by this proposed action, and a group of leading intellectuals, including André Malraux (1901–76), Jean-Paul Sartre and Louis Aragon (1897–1982), prepared and signed a statement against the executions. The idea was that the statement would be taken to Spain and read out at a press conference, or some other type of event, to publicize the action that the Franco government was contemplating. It was eventually decided to select a group of people to fly to Madrid and to arrange a press conference. Michel Foucault, the film director Costa-Gavras (1933–) and the actor and singer Yves Montand (1921–91) were selected, among others, to go to Madrid. They were allowed entry to Spain, perhaps because the authorities were unaware of their precise intentions. They just managed to read out their brief document when the police arrived to arrest them. They were escorted back to the airport and put on a flight back to Paris. At the small press conference and at the airport there were confrontations between the police and the presenters of the petition. It is perhaps easy to think of this action as a small political gesture by well-known figures, but it did carry an element of risk. It was by no means impossible that Foucault and his colleagues could have been detained at a police station or even prison, and subjected to quite harsh treatment. Spain at the time was a fascist dictatorship and the government appeared to care little for external public or political opinion and had a less than desirable human rights record. It demanded considerable courage to challenge the government on its own soil in such a confrontational way. The incident reveals an aspect of Foucault's character that came to light at varying times in his career – his fortitude and determination to face up to oppression wherever he saw it.

By 1976 there was also growing international concern about the position of political dissidents in the Soviet Union. It was particularly difficult for dissidents or for members of their family to leave the USSR, and Foucault campaigned vigorously for such people. It sometimes left Foucault and other intellectuals in a rather difficult position in terms of their support for Marxist ideas. As a broad principle, intellectuals had tended to look to left-wing ideas for an ideology that could be used to counteract those of right-wing governments and their perceived random exercise of power. To some extent, it was natural to look to the Soviet Union for such an alternative ideology. However, the stories emerging from the Soviet Union under Leonid Brezhnev appeared to suggest a country suffering under an oppressive regime. It was, in a sense, a real challenge to the left-wing or communist ideologies of intellectuals in the West.

Insight

Left-wing intellectuals in the West were drawn to the Soviet Union for ideological reasons, but were increasingly confronted by what was increasingly being revealed as a totalitarian regime and its human rights abuses. This was a thorny problem for many left-wing thinkers and writers in the post-war period.

It was therefore a time when academics and writers were searching for an alternative world view that could be used to combat the inequalities and oppression that they saw in the West, yet which did not specifically draw upon Marxist ideas. In 1977 Brezhnev came on a visit to Paris, which was the occasion for numerous demonstrations against the treatment of dissidents in the USSR. Foucault was involved in some of these and concentrated his attentions on protesting against the abuse of human rights. His protests therefore tended to adopt the moral high ground, and to focus upon the ethical issue of the manner in which opponents of the Soviet system were treated.

It is also interesting that Foucault appeared to be adopting a strongly ethical argument in relation to other issues. In 1977 one of the lawyers for the left-wing terrorist group known as the Red Army Faction sought asylum in France, and the issue caused considerable public debate. Some individuals and groups made statements in support of the lawyer, and also directly or implicitly in favour of terrorism in combating what they saw as state oppression in the West. Foucault would not involve himself in statements supporting terrorism, and restricted himself to support for the lawyer. There were again demonstrations, and again Foucault took part in some of them, even receiving physical injuries during confrontations with the police. It does appear that in these political demonstrations Foucault tended to adopt generally non-violent means, and limited himself to simply stating his case.

Insight

At this time Foucault entered energetically into the debate about the extent to which the state should take action against those who expressed opinions against its policies. Foucault sometimes expressed this issue in terms of the way in which society sees 'truth'. In other words, Foucault saw there as being an important debate about how the state viewed the nature of truth about a situation, and how pressure groups viewed that same situation.

International politics

In early 1978 considerable world attention was being focused on Iran, and the opposition to the established government of Shah Mohammad Reza Pahlavi. The pro-Western government of Iran was coming under increasing pressure from an Islamic-inspired opposition that sought to replace the existing regime with a government committed to Islamic principles. Foucault became very interested in this development and in late 1978 was asked by the Italian newspaper *Corriere della Sera* to write some articles analysing the situation in Iran. To this end, Foucault visited Iran in September 1978 to collect data for his articles. In addition, during the next few months he also published articles in the French press. Foucault was particularly interested that 'uprisings have so easily found their expression and their drama in religious forms' (Faubion, *Michel Foucault: Power*, p. 450).

The government of the Shah had been in power in Iran since the 1940s and had been consistently supported by the United States, which feared Soviet expansionism in the area. The Iranian government had always adopted policies that were aligned with the West, and favoured a secular state rather than one inspired by traditional Islamic principles. There had always been opposition to the Shah's rule, particularly from the Islamic clergy and those in favour of a return to religious principles. Very little real opposition was, however, permitted within the country and the government tried to suppress any significant dissent. Most opposition to the Shah was centred around a leading religious figure, the Ayatollah Khomeini. During the 1960s he had regularly opposed the government, calling for a return to Islamic principles in the country. The government had finally exiled him from the country because of his opposition to the Shah.

By 1977 there was a sense that the opposition to the Shah was growing in impetus, and in various parts of the country there were demonstrations and protests against his rule. In 1978 there were demonstrations in the cities of Qum and Tabriz, and demonstrators were killed by government forces. There were also attacks on Western-oriented institutions. Throughout the year the protests increased in frequency and intensity. On 8 September there was a major protest in the centre of Tehran, and government forces opened fire on the demonstrators in an attempt to maintain order. It was, however, a vain attempt because by now there was a sense that the overthrow of the government was inevitable, even though it was difficult to predict how this would take place. There was so many injuries and deaths among the demonstrators on 8 September that it was termed 'Black Friday'.

It was shortly after this event, that Foucault arrived in Tehran. This initial visit was followed by another in November, and hence Foucault was present in Iran during the height of the protests against the Shah. At this stage, Ayatollah Khomeini was in exile in Iraq, but he shortly moved to France, where he stayed in a suburb of Paris. Protests continued to expand throughout December 1978, and finally, after some negotiation with opposition groups, the Shah and his family left Iran in mid-January 1979. In February, Ayatollah Khomeini returned from France and received a rapturous welcome from opposition groups. He consolidated his power during the next few months and gradually established a government rooted in Islamic principles. The new government did, however, come under some international criticism for its human rights abuses, especially its persecution of those who had connections with the Shah's regime. There were also criticisms of the new judicial system and of the regime's treatment of women.

In his journalism Foucault was, from the beginning, very critical of the Shah's regime. He saw it as autocratic, particularly in terms of its use of a secret police as a means to establish a climate of fear among the population. He tended to be very enthusiastic about the opposition of Ayatollah Khomeini, viewing it as potentially ushering in a new form of religious democracy. He seems, however, to have overlooked or not accepted alternative analyses that saw the potential both for totalitarianism and the oppression of women within the proposed religious state.

Insight

It is difficult to understand exactly why Foucault was relatively enthusiastic about the regime of Ayatollah Khomeini. Perhaps he felt that a regime that subscribed to religious principles would be in harmony with the Western principles of human rights. He may also have felt that Western democracies were not in any case perfect in this regard, and that the new regime would be no worse. Certainly, however, Foucault's position lost him considerable credibility among his former supporters.

He listened to the arguments put forward by supporters of Khomeini, that men and women, would be treated differently but equally in a new religious state. He seemed to have accepted the principle that it was possible to treat men and women by different standards, and yet to retain a principle of equality between the sexes. It may be that, when he heard people predicting an oppressive regime that would reduce drastically the liberty of women in particular, he felt that people were being unnecessarily critical of Islamic society. Foucault predicted that, in a country led by the ayatollahs, there would not be any form of hierarchy, and thus the country would tend towards democracy. In this he seems to have underestimated not only the power of the ayatollahs, but their desire to use this power to control the religious nature of the new society. Foucault seems to have thought that the Islamic clerics would not use their authority to determine the behaviour of citizens in the new Iran. He seemed to think that the society would return to a form of benign ideal characteristic of the society during the lifetime of the Prophet Muhammad. There were grave concerns among some during late 1978 and early 1979 that the lives of minority groups such as the Baha'is would be in danger from an Islamic society. Foucault did not think this was at all likely; but unfortunately events would prove him wrong.

Some women, both within and outside Iran, began to speak against the proposed regime, once they realized that there was a possibility of an Islamic government. They were concerned about the possibility of a 'fundamentalist' ideology, and also that a new religious administration would in effect retain the worst excesses of the previous regime, albeit supported by different justifications. Those who spoke out were also fearful of the forms of Islamic judicial punishment that they saw in other Islamic countries. Foucault had in effect, in his earlier journalism, suggested that the idea of linking religion and politics could produce a very effective type of government. This idea was severely criticized by a number of political writers in France. Moreover, it soon became clear that other minorities were in serious danger in Iran, and stories emerged of the executions of homosexuals.

One area of Foucault's writing on Iran appears to be particularly inconsistent. Throughout the rest of his research and writing, Foucault was consistent in arguing against the idea of all-embracing world views that sought to explain everything within society. In a personal sense, he seemed to want to retain his personal freedom to interpret society as he wished, and also to retain that freedom of thought for others. He did not wish to be constrained within a single paradigm or theoretical perspective. Yet, in his writing about Iran, he did not appear to feel that there was any danger of totalitarianism within the religious regime of the ayatollahs. This was despite the many voices raised in concern outside Iran, and the extensive evidence emerging from the country. As this evidence accumulated, particularly in relation to the treatment of women, Foucault did not noticeably withdraw any of his statements or arguments about Iran, and this caused some surprise among those who counted themselves as supporters of Foucault's thought and writing. He did, however, continue to campaign on human rights issues.

One of Foucault's most significant campaigns was that designed to amass support for the 'boat people' who were leaving Vietnam from the late 1970s onwards. The fall of Saigon in April 1975, to the North Vietnamese army, witnessed the beginning of a series of attempts by many people to leave the former South Vietnam to seek refuge in other neighbouring countries, or if possible, to be granted asylum in countries such as the United States or Australia. People wanted to leave the former South Vietnam because either they had been involved with working for the American administration and hence would be subject to reprisals, or were likely to be placed in internment camps because they were ideologically opposed to North Vietnam. The years after the victory of the North Vietnamese and the reunification of the country, were very uncertain times for many people, until the country as a whole had been stabilized after many years of warfare. Many people had great difficulty in finding a means of leaving Vietnam, and many had recourse to buying a place in a boat that would try to reach friendly shores or make contact with a larger vessel in international waters. The so-called 'boat people' who attempted this dangerous method of escaping from Vietnam suffered considerably. Many boats were unfit to venture out into the ocean and capsized; while some of the boats were captured by pirates who robbed the refugees of their few worldly possessions and often murdered them, too. Some, however, were fortunate enough to be rescued by large ships and granted asylum in Western countries. The dangers faced by Vietnamese refugees began to attract media attention, particularly in France owing to that country's previous colonial involvement with Vietnam. Foucault made consistent and determined efforts to keep the issue in the media, and to try to ensure that as much as possible was done to give practical help to those seeking to escape from Vietnam.

Foucault was thus widely involved in causes that had a political dimension, yet which were primarily concerned with trying to defend human rights in a variety of ways. Although he was generally connected in these activities with people on the left of the political spectrum, he always seemed to try to avoid adopting a particular ideological position himself. He seemed to wish to avoid being labelled as a 'left-wing' intellectual, although the causes that he espoused could be broadly categorized by many as being within these broad parameters. Foucault may well be remembered for the vigour with which he tried to defend the fundamental rights of those who tended to have rather less influence and power in society.

10 THINGS TO REMEMBER

1 *In 1950 Foucault joined the French Communist Party, perhaps influenced by the ideas of the philosopher Louis Althusser, a lecturer at the Ecole normale supérieure.*

2 *Foucault appeared to have considerable doubts about being a member of an organization that would implicitly require him to adopt a particular ideological position on issues in society.*

3 *He appears to have become particularly active in political terms at about the time of the 1968 student protests in Paris.*

4 *As a result of the 1968 protests, the French government established a new experimental university at Vincennes, and Foucault was invited to be the head of the Department of Philosophy.*

5 *In 1969 student protests continued at Vincennes, and Foucault was involved in these.*

6 *In 1970 Foucault was elected as a professor at arguably the leading academic institution in France, the Collège de France.*

7 *Foucault established the Groupe d'information sur les prisons, which sought to collect data on the conditions in French prisons, with a view to acting as a pressure group to improve conditions.*

8 *In 1975 he drew public attention to the proposed execution by the Franco regime in Spain of political opponents.*

9 *In 1978 Foucault was employed as a journalist to report on the events in Iran that led to the Iranian Revolution.*

10 *After the victory of North Vietnam against South Vietnam, and the exodus of the United States army, a number of Vietnamese people tried to leave Vietnam by boat, often losing their lives in the process. Foucault tried to draw international attention to the situation of the 'boat people'.*

8

The nature of institutions

In this chapter you will learn about:
- *Foucault's analysis of the nature of social and political institutions*
- *the power relationship between institutions and the individual*
- *Foucault's observations on the nature of truth and discourse within institutions.*

The rise of institutions

A theme to which Foucault frequently returned was that of the power of institutions to influence the lives of individuals in society. One of the significant developments of postmodern society has been the expansion of institutions whether these be in the private or public sector. Such institutions have frequently also become global in their structures and influence. Banks, for example, have long been international in their influence, but in other sectors, such as energy production, countries buy and sell energy in such complex ways that we may not be sure where the energy we use has been generated. In addition, institutions have become much more diverse in terms of the services that they offer. Supermarkets can now act as banks, while banks themselves provide additional services such as insurance.

The sheer complexity and diversity of the services provided by institutions can result in the individual becoming dependent upon the institution. This can happen in a variety of ways.

First, institutions group services together in a way that may be initially attractive to the individual. The latter may be offered discounts, for example, to take out loans, or to purchase house maintenance services, travel insurance or tickets from either one institution or from groups of linked institutions. This may be appealing initially, as it appears to be easier to go to just one institution. However, one may not necessarily receive the same degree of specialist help and advice that one would receive from separate, specialist institutions. Moreover, through systems such as this where the individual obtains a group of services from the same institution, he or she, it could be argued, loses a certain degree of autonomy. There is a tendency to remain with the one institution rather than making enquiries with separate institutions. Foucault was very conscious of the danger that institutions posed for the loss of the autonomy of individuals.

Insight

In the modern age, before the advent of computers, society remained relatively straightforward. However, in a high-tech, postmodern age the great diversity of services on offer can be bewildering. It is not easy for the individual to cope with the range of consumer possibilities, and it is thus tempting to rely on a single organization to provide these.

Another facet of the way in which contemporary institutions function occurs when different aspects of the same service are operated by different companies. This happens for example in the travel industry where different aspects of the process are managed by different institutions. This can lead to doubt in the mind of the individual about which aspects are controlled by which company. Confusion may then arise if the individual wishes to make a claim for some part of the service. This again can result in a loss of the autonomy of the individual because he or she is unsure about the location of responsibility.

This increasing complexity of institutions is evident in all sectors from health to education, and has to some extent been generated by a philosophy of consumer choice. This is a persuasive doctrine that superficially at least appears to increase the freedom of individuals. However, it is difficult to broaden individual choice in relation to consumer services without at the same time increasing the complexity of provision. That very complexity then often results in the individual finding it very difficult to understand the choices available. In other words, it may become a self-defeating philosophy. The very complexity of institutions thus can make individuals dependent upon them, simply because they are so difficult to understand. Furthermore, there is a tendency in postmodern society to seek security, whether this be provided by enhanced medical care or by insurance provision. In some ways institutions appear to offer security, and yet this is negated by the lack of confidence that may be felt in the complexity of organizations. One might argue that the complexity of society has in many ways reduced the autonomy of individuals.

Foucault argued that there are two competing tendencies in relation to autonomy and institutions. Some people are able to cope with the complexity of organizations and to take advantage of the autonomy resulting from diversity of choice, while others find this problematic. Diversity has often been related to the electronic and digital nature of developments in organizations. So many services are now available online, and indeed may be exclusively available online, that only those with a facility in computing can access them. Yet not everyone in society may have the resources, financial or otherwise, to access Internet provision. Hence, although computerization has democratized access to information in many ways, it has also produced barriers to understanding and taking advantage of the facilities provided by institutions. Foucault pointed out that there are sectors of society that are excluded from access to the functions of institutions because of their inability either to understand the complexity of organizations, or the medium of transmission of information.

Institutions and the state

The complexity of institutions also has another effect noted by Foucault, and that is the sense of alienation that results when people cannot understand the power and authority exerted by institutions. Organizations now typically are controlled by, or regulate themselves through, a highly complex, quasi-legal set of procedures. These are sometimes very difficult to understand, even by people who work every day within the institution, but even more so by those external to the organization. Hence, when an individual appeals to an institution for a decision, it is often difficult to understand the grounds upon which that decision has been made. If the decision appears to be unfair, or does not take into account the circumstances of the individual, then this may appear to be particularly alienating. As Foucault pointed out, under these circumstances the individual can feel very disenchanted and disempowered by the authority of an organization.

Insight

Foucault already appreciated the trend towards the greater and greater legal-bureaucratic nature of organizations. This trend has only been compounded by the all-pervasive use of information technology. Even more, the rapidly changing nature of IT has made it difficult for the ordinary consumer to understand the mechanisms in place.

Throughout his life Foucault tended to be opposed to large organizations and institutions, and also to large-scale state power, because he felt these types of decision-making removed personal autonomy. He felt that the hiatus between the state as an institution, and the disempowered individual, was too great. Foucault's solution was to decentralize the loci of power so that they were much closer to the consumers of the services and decisions produced by the state. In this way, when individuals participated in decision-making, the resultant decisions had a much more immediate effect upon the lives of those individuals.

It is worthwhile, however, looking at the situation from the point of view of the institution. It is probably reasonable to argue that many people do not fully appreciate the rapidity of the changes that are taking place in the environments in which institutions function. The contemporary world is characterized by extremely rapid social change, and institutions have to change rapidly themselves in order to cope with the transformation of society. One of the results of this is that institutions may not be able to provide the type of services to which individuals have become accustomed over the years. This can again lead to alienation among clients and consumers. Institutions are subject to economic, social and political changes in society, which impose a continual requirement on them to respond and to reflect these changes in their own systems. Individuals may sometimes have expectations of institutions that relate to periods in which the economic and political environment was different.

For Foucault, however, the principal ideological conflict was between large institutions and the state on the one hand, and the individual members of the electorate on the other. Foucault considered that society needed to be in a continual state of reflection and change in order to cope with this ideological opposition, and that ideas for change were likely to be more suitable and appropriate if they emerged from the individuals in society rather than from institutions. The individual was more likely to be able to identify tensions in society, and the possible solutions which would be likely to generate improvements. This was largely because the individual was closer to the problems of society, and could perceive more clearly the consequences of the strategies which were implemented.

Insight

Although there is much discussion about devolution of power in Western society, and the virtues of localized decision-making, much power would still appear to be centralized. Foucault tried to argue that power was much more distributed than we might imagine, although this was not necessarily congruent with peoples' experience.

For Foucault, the relationship between all institutions and either individual employees or individual citizens was one of power. He also extended this notion to apply to all relationships between human beings where he considered that ultimately one individual would emerge in a position of power and the other or others in a subservient position. He did not consider that this was of itself necessarily undesirable. One might argue that it is of the nature of human beings that some people naturally assume power and the role of decision-makers. One might also further argue that this is desirable to the extent that it is an effective form of decision-making. However, Foucault also considered that there were undesirable aspects of this continual emergence of power as an element of human relationships. Once power emerges as an element in relationships, whether institutional or personal, it tends to work in opposition to the emergence of collegiate, cooperative relationships. Instead of working together democratically, trying to resolve issues collaboratively, one person tends to assume dominance and tries to impose his or her will on the other.

Institutions and social provision

Foucault took as an example the provision of social services and medicine in society, and argued that there were inherent points of conflict resulting from intrinsic power relationships. He firstly pointed out two arguments that have become frequently debated in terms of the provision of health and medicine. It is verifiable empirically that society continues to make considerable advances in the understanding of medical conditions as well as in their treatment. The extent of medical research is such that advances in medical understanding continue to make rapid progress, with some of these advances being made because of research in the public sector, and some because of research in the private sector (for example, in large pharmaceutical companies). However, the theoretically limitless advance in medical knowledge results in more and more expensive treatments, the funding of which is problematic for society. We are now well used to the idea that health providers have to make decisions about which treatments they will routinely provide, and which treatments, although available, cannot be financed within existing resources. This situation highlights Foucault's arguments about the existence of power relations between institutions and individuals. Health providers no doubt need to be able to make decisions about the distribution of resources and, moreover, are required by society to do so. Nevertheless this introduces a conflictual situation where an individual human being is told that he or she cannot access treatment for one condition, whereas another individual can access treatment for a different condition. The individual is rarely happy about a situation where an institution can exercise this kind of power. Of course, those who are successful in obtaining treatment may feel more accepting of the system in the short term, but they will be only too aware that in different circumstances the situation may not have developed to their advantage.

Insight

In health care, complex ethical dilemmas develop where the availability of limited resources has to be balanced against the medical needs of patients. There are frequently many different variables in such circumstances, including the age of patients, the likely prognosis of different illnesses, the cost and difficulty of treatment, and the availability of specialists.

Ultimately, as Foucault pointed out, the increase in medical knowledge has led to a situation where people have greater and greater expectations of a health system that does not unfortunately have the financial resources to meet those expectations. As more and more medical conditions are brought within the scope of those that are potentially treatable, it will become increasingly difficult to meet the expectations of patients. Such a situation will inevitably lead to disenchantment among members of society with regard to the institutions that have the power to distribute resources.

This dichotomy between the perceived needs of individuals and the ability of institutions to satisfy them raises important ethical questions. On the one hand, there is the question of the moral responsibility of the state or of institutions to safeguard the health or broader welfare of individuals. Ultimately, of course, one could argue that the state and its institutions cannot ensure that its citizens are healthy, just as it cannot ensure that they are intelligent, well educated, or have lots of friends. So much depends for the acquisition of these qualities on both genetic and environmental factors, and also on such factors as personality and motivation. Nevertheless, one might argue that the state institutions do have a moral responsibility to establish the infrastructure in order to enable citizens to enhance, for example, their own health and education. In other words, on this argument, the state should provide a system of schools, and a system of health diagnosis and treatment, even though this cannot ultimately guarantee that a person will be either well educated or healthy.

The more complex ethical questions arise when the state institutions do have the potential to provide services but decline to provide them freely, through lack of financial resources. For example, an individual may have the entry requirements for access to a postgraduate course in a university, but cannot afford the course fees. Alternatively, a medical facility has the potential to provide treatment to an individual but decides that it cannot provide the treatment unless substantial fees are paid. The moral and practical question becomes whether the individual can reasonably expect a state institution to intervene on all occasions.

Insight

The individual citizen becomes alienated in a situation where it appears evident that the state does have the resources to provide health care, but chooses not to do so. The individual is usually all too well aware that the state has spent money on defence, transport infrastructure, or law and order, yet what they are really concerned about is their own health and the need for treatment.

Foucault argued that the individual could have reasonable expectations that institutions would not create adverse conditions for the individual that might, for example, affect their health or their education or general welfare. For example, an industrial company should not pollute the environment in such a way as to damage the health of citizens and society should maintain an adequate level of purity of water supplies for its citizens. In other words, the general infrastructure of society should be maintained in order to sustain a reasonable quality of life for individuals. Foucault considered, however, that one could not have a definite view on exactly the way in which this related to individual needs. He felt that it was extremely difficult to make the transition from discussing general principles of societal provision, to the way in which society should address the specific demands and needs of individuals.

Foucault appeared to argue that ultimately there was no rational way in which this problem might be resolved. However, he considered that the decision-making interface was the area to which attention should be addressed. It was important, he considered, that the boundaries of what could be provided in terms of services by society and institutions should be continually addressed. These boundaries should be regularly defined and redefined in a transparent way. There should not be an expectation that these boundaries could remain fixed and unmoving, but at least the decision-making process should be clear to everyone. The criteria for decision-making should be clearly stated in order that individual citizens can be aware of the basis of arguments and decisions.

Traditionally there was the assumption that there was a form of pact, written or unwritten, between the individual and the state. The latter, explicitly or implicitly, agreed to safeguard the health and welfare of the individual, in exchange for the individual's loyalty and agreement to abide by the laws of the state. The latter even extended to an agreement to take up arms to defend the state if this was required. However, Foucault thought that, in a modern world, various considerations, notably economic factors, undermined the capacity of the state institutions to adhere to this contract, and to protect its citizens in all respects. There were simply not the economic resources available to assure the health and welfare of citizens in all cases. This applied in a variety of contexts, including for example, the care of the elderly or in the provision of housing. There were thus enormous moral questions in such a situation about the responsibility of institutions. Equally, if institutions could no longer provide a level of care for the individual, then, in a sense, the pact between state and individual broke down. The individual might no longer be prepared to give his or her loyalty to the state, and the result could be a form of societal breakdown, where the unwritten rules of loyalty and responsibility to society crumbled away.

> ## Insight
> The notion of a contract between citizen and state is an important factor in maintaining the cohesion of society. Without such a contract, trust breaks down and citizens lose faith in the different functions of society, such as the capacity of the state to maintain law and order.

Institutions and contemporary society

Foucault raised the question of how we can be sure of the nature of present-day postmodern society. He noted that it was difficult to ensure that one understood the basis upon which decisions were made or even when decisions had been taken in society. He addressed the question of 'truth' and the ways in which we might purport to know the truth of a society. In more specific terms, he noted that state decision-making was rarely transparent, and that decisions were obscured by a variety of means. Institutions and professional groups took numerous decisions about how to treat people, or the services with which to provide people, without making clear the way in which they reached those decisions. Foucault argued that, if the foundations of those decisions, or even the fact that the decisions were made in the first place, were made public, then there could well be serious public opposition.

Foucault was interested in the concept of 'strategy' or, in the sense that he used the term, the means employed by institutions to exert their power and authority over the individual. In postmodern society one of the features of institutions is a growing complexity of administrative systems. This was enabled both by the increasing complexity of financial systems available but principally by the use of computers and electronic means of communication. It has been possible, for example, to diversify considerably the means by which services are offered to consumers, and to arrange that in some cases the only means of accessing services is by computer. In addition, this reliance upon computer systems enables organizations to offer an extremely sophisticated range of services that in some cases are extremely complicated to access. The services are so complex, not only intrinsically but also in the manner in which they are provided, that the individual is often confused by the sheer diversity of provision. This gives the institution a form of power over the individual, and while it may or may not be a deliberate strategy in all situations, the result of such systems of organization is often an increased power for the organization.

A significant element of this increased complexity of systems is that it tends to favour those individuals who are familiar with electronic systems of communication and also with computer systems. It also remains true that there is a significant group in society that either does not have easy access to computers, or remains non computer-literate. In such cases, they simply cannot take advantage of these new institutional systems. The unequal distribution of such knowledge and skills thus disadvantages certain sectors of the community.

In a modern society, power relations are often reinforced by the selective acquisition of knowledge. However, one result of computerization has been to make knowledge, for example of the law and of medicine, more accessible. The increased availability of knowledge, it can be argued, has resulted in a diminution of authority for the professions and related institutions. It has become possible for ordinary citizens to challenge the knowledge and decisions of professionals. With the reduction in the authority and power of institutions, associated with the possession of knowledge, has come a parallel rise in power associated with a complexity of systems. It is theoretically possible for institutions to manipulate bureaucratic systems to make one set of choices relatively straightforward to make, while a different set of choices may be far more complex to access. The result is that it may be possible for institutions to encourage individuals to make one set of choices rather than another.

In Foucault's terms, institutions are continually seeking ways of controlling individuals who are inherently free and autonomous. Indeed he argues that there is, in a sense, a logical impossibility of the use of power by institutions, unless those against whom the power is exercised are in fact autonomous. In other words, power is concerned with the influencing of the behaviour of individuals. There is here the basis for a fundamental conflict between the institution and the individual. The latter wishes to retain his or her freedom of action, while the former wishes to constrain it.

Insight

Foucault, like Sartre, was interested in the concept of freedom. Foucault was interested in analysing the various strategies employed by institutions in order to limit the freedom of the individual, and make ordinary citizens more compliant and willing to align their behaviour with the needs of the state.

Foucault did not view the relationship between institution and individual as being one of outright conflict and antagonism, but rather one in which the institution seeks to control the behaviour of the individual. In other words, it is more a relationship where the institution attempts to manipulate the collective behaviour of individuals. Foucault attempted to distinguish between violent acts that are always directed towards people, and the exercise of power that tends to be directed towards the actions of other people. Violence, for Foucault, attempts to subdue a person or organism, and to render them incapable of carrying out a series of actions. On the other hand, the use of power attempts to amend the ways in which individuals act, so that their actions are more amenable to the policies or politics of the institution.

During the modern period, the purpose of institutions, according to Foucault, has not been to generate obedience on the part of individuals, but rather to encourage individuals to behave in a more rational way that meets the needs of the institution.

Yet another feature of institutions in the postmodern world has been their quasi-legal infrastructure and systems. Institutions tend to create systems of regulations and rules that control many aspects of the way in which they conduct themselves, not dissimilar to the legal systems created by governments. Indeed, a detailed knowledge of such regulatory frameworks constitutes a form of power because it can be used to specify what an employee may or may not do. Equally well, the emphasis upon quality assurance enhances the regulatory framework. Quality systems, among other things, specify the way in which documents must be produced, the way in which procedures are analysed in order to be considered valid or invalid, and the way in which new systems are added to the general infrastructure. New systems cannot be employed, or simply used to enhance the existing infrastructure, without being subjected to some form of approval.

Thus certain forms of communication are defined by an institution as valid and true, and become accepted by the individuals who are subject to that institution. These forms of communication and discourse are characterized in a variety of ways. First, certain concepts are designated by the institution as being of significance – for example 'evaluation' or 'customer satisfaction'. Evaluation forms are distributed to clients and a great emphasis may be placed on the results. The data gathered from them may be regarded as 'true', despite the many methodological problems with the collection and analysis of such data. When evaluation questionnaires are distributed to people, there is often no control over the manner in which they are completed, and hence over the truth or validity of the data. One person may devote a great deal of time and thought to completing the questionnaire, whereas another may make rapid, spontaneous responses. Despite the uncertainties of the methodology, if an institution decides to place an emphasis upon the discourse of evaluation, then such surveys become very important, for example in determining the value of different employees to the institution. Those who receive good evaluations become valued by the organization, and those who receive less complimentary evaluations may be regarded as of less value to the institution. Thus the form of discourse in an institution can be directly related to the exercise of power, through the means of that which is considered as true.

The concept of truth in institutions is problematic to the extent that some aspects of discourse and communication may be considered as reflecting an absolute truth when in fact they reflect only a provisional attempt at defining what took place. Institutions use a variety of strategies to try to determine and record the truth of events. Meetings, for example, are recorded as 'minutes', which at a later date become 'accepted' as a valid record of the meeting. Of course, minutes represent a selection of the events and opinions expressed at the meeting. They are a subjective record of the events, reflecting the perceptions of the writer, rather than a concept of absolute truth. Moreover, the normal time delay in validating minutes often results in the latter being accepted simply because those who were present cannot remember with certainty anything different. Yet such minutes become accepted as the reality of the institution. They are used in a variety of ways in terms of developing policy or resolving disputes. In short, then, the 'truth' of institutions is inevitably a reflection of the subjectivity of those who are part of this social construction.

Foucault pointed out that, even though the systems of institutions are often highly rational, this does not mean that they are fair or democratic, or that they give rise to a use of power that is desirable. For example, the committee structure of an institution may be rational, and organized in a manner that appears to support a democratic structure, yet decision-making in those committees may be far from democratic. The reality may be that some people dominate the committees and exercise considerable influence over the decision-making processes. In other words, rational procedures that use legal-bureaucratic systems may not in fact encourage the development of a validity or an adherence to truth that one might have expected. Foucault noted the legal-rational system may be used by institutions that are exploitative or that exercise undue power over individuals.

For Foucault, one of the most important achievements of an institution was to dedicate itself to the pursuit of truth. Institutions should always avoid, according to Foucault, making the assumption that they have access to the truth, for this could lead to a situation where those who did not have a similar view of truth were marginalized. Foucault argued that the pursuit of truth was a continual process of seeking, rather than arrival at, a particular view of the world.

Insight

This approach to the nature of truth was in keeping with Foucault's role as a social science researcher. The prevalent perspective in social science is that truth is not an absolute, but is a process whereby one gets closer and closer to a more accurate model of reality.

Foucault argued that the way in which institutions exerted power and authority over individuals was not ultimately through economic and political systems, but by means of a form of rationality. In other words, it involved the way in which the institution was structured and organized. One of the most important facets of this is the way in which the organization justifies its actions and priorities. There are, suggested Foucault, those 'charged with saying what counts as true' (Gordon, *Michel Foucault: Power/Knowledge*, p. 131). It has become normal for institutions to develop mission statements that outline the key priorities of the institution. Such statements have the effect of setting priorities that exert power over individuals by means of determining those who will, or will not, be perceived as successful.

Foucault had a particular concept of analysing issues and problems, and of trying to approach the truth. He started to write a book or article about an issue before he had actually thought out his position very clearly about the research issue under question. In other words, the writing of a book for Foucault was a form of experiment – a type of empirical and conceptual enquiry. He analysed the issue or problem as he wrote the book. His thinking about the subject was thus influenced by the process of reflecting upon it. There was thus in Foucault a type of reflexive process. There was a continual process of interaction between Foucault analysing the question at hand, and the issue being analysed having an influence upon Foucault. In a sense, this is a form of circular argument, with each circle influencing previous circles, and also the circular reasoning patterns to come. Each of Foucault's books is thus an experiment, the results of which are relatively unpredictable.

In terms of his vision of unravelling the 'truth' of a situation or of a research question, Foucault was not really a social scientist. He did not set out to either test a theory through deduction, or to generate a new theory by means of induction. His was a much more personal, subjective and exploratory journey. When confronted by a research problem, he set out to examine it and to interact with the issue in a subjective way, leading to a kind of transformation of both the problem and his own thinking processes about the issue. One might perhaps describe his approach as a subjective psychological approach, rather than objective social science.

For Foucault, one of the problems of institutions, and in particular perhaps educational institutions, is that they operate according to a fairly fixed and rigid world view, which constrains those who either work within them or interact with them. Financial institutions or companies in the Western world operate within a paradigm of free-market capitalism, which determines the processes and procedures that they use and also their aims. Although it may appear that educational institutions are paradigm-free, this was not the case according to Foucault. They subscribe to a particular way of doing science, a particular way of analysing issues conceptually, and a particular way of writing about research. Universities may have, for example, a particular way of thinking about philosophy in terms of analysing the way words are used in order to reveal something of the significance of concepts. On the other hand, philosophy may be employed to try to explore the nature of human existence, and the purposes to which we put our lives. The academic world has also defined certain preferred methods of writing about research and enquiry, notably the academic journal article. Yet this method of recording research does have drawbacks. The length of the journal article does not permit the effective presentation of data, and discussions of methodological issues are often very limited. Nevertheless, it is accepted as the desirable method and is widely used. In many ways, Foucault would like to discard these paradigmatic approaches and to develop new methodologies and approaches as and when they become necessary.

There is, of course, a methodological problem with this, which is that the continual development of new methodologies makes it very difficult to validate a specific approach to research. The virtue of operating within an agreed and consistent paradigm is that at least it facilitates a form of discourse within agreed limits and according to agreed conventions. 'Truth' is always truth within a particular conceptual framework, a particular way of looking at the world. This is the reason for relative difficulty experienced by Foucault in speaking about valid truth, because the parameters within which he examined it were always changing. Nevertheless, Foucault maintained his opposition to the study of the great systems of thought represented by the study of the history of ideas. He opposed this approach to philosophy because he considered it a regimented approach to understanding the world that did not provide sufficient flexibility for the fresh analysis of ideas.

Although Foucault was in some ways a very academic and scholarly writer, he was also in other ways the antithesis of the scholarly academic. He did not, for example, hold the view that academic research alone was sufficient to understand the social world and its problems. Foucault considered that ultimately it was necessary to talk to people about their experiences of the world, and that this direct appreciation of people's experiences provided a more valid approach to 'truth'. The two approaches of academic research and of informal interviews could of course be combined in a variety of qualitative research approaches including ethnographic or phenomenological research, or biographical or life history approaches.

10 THINGS TO REMEMBER

1 *Foucault was interested in exploring the ways in which institutions exerted influence and authority over individuals.*

2 *Some people are in effect excluded from the services provided by institutions because they cannot understand the mechanisms by which they operate.*

3 *Foucault argued that, when people cannot understand the way in which institutions exercise power over them, they can become alienated.*

4 *Foucault tended to be opposed to large institutions and also to state power because he believed that they undermined personal autonomy.*

5 *He noted the inherent conflicts in the provision of health care, where resource capacity sometimes limited the provision of treatment.*

6 *Foucault pointed out that there was sometimes a conflict between the perceived needs of people and the capacity of the state to meet those needs.*

7 *He argued that there was an implicit contract between the individual and the state, such that the individual would have a loyalty to the needs of the state, while at the same time the state would protect the individual citizen.*

8 *Foucault felt that it was not possible for institutions to have an absolute concept of truth, but only to be able to construct a provisional model of the world.*

(Contd)

9   *Foucault applied this principle to the writing of books, where he considered that the process of writing was a form of research and enquiry whereby he gained greater understanding of an issue through the very process of writing about it.*

10 *Foucault was opposed to adopting a specific ideological position because it tended to lead to the notion of an absolute truth about an issue.*

9

The role of the intellectual

In this chapter you will learn about:
- *the role of the intellectual in society*
- *Foucault's concept of his own role as an intellectual*
- *the different aspects of Foucault's contribution to society as an intellectual.*

The concept of the intellectual

The intellectual in Europe has probably been generally perceived as someone on the left of centre in political terms, who analyses political events from a broadly socialist viewpoint, and who passes judgement on such events for a mass readership. This is no doubt a rather stereotypical view of the intellectual's role, and probably not representative of a number of writers and political analysts. Yet there is an element in it which is certainly reminiscent of writers such as Sartre who could probably legitimately be described as intellectuals. An element of this stereotypical view of the intellectual was also that he or she was a philosopher who attempted a philosophical or sociological analysis of the position of human beings in relation to the great institutions of society, and who attempted to suggest ways in which the individual might address the great questions of the purpose of life and existence.

Foucault noted that there had been a trend towards intellectuals specializing in specific areas of society rather than commenting upon broader universal themes. Foucault argues that formerly the writer was the archetypal intellectual, able to comment on a very wide range of issues, often political or social, and to analyse them from a variety of perspectives. However, with the great diversification of the media of communication in postmodern society, this has changed somewhat. When comments are required on television programmes from 'experts' in a particular field, it is often university lecturers, rather than writers per se, who are asked to provide analyses. These lecturers, as Foucault commented, are usually specialists in a particular field of knowledge or practice. An advantage of this situation is that it is usually possible to obtain detailed and well-informed specialist comment on issues, drawing from the research expertise available in higher education. Nevertheless, what we might term the 'generalist intellectual' was perhaps able to provide a better contextual comment, to the extent that he or she was well versed in a variety of fields of thought.

The rise in the scale and significance of the academic world, and of the expansion of the university system, resulted in the writer, and indeed his or her writing, being absorbed within the academic system. The result of this was the transformation of intellectual writing into academic writing, with all the conventions such as detailed references and footnotes that are typical of the genre. To some extent, writers, in addition, came to be judged by their academic qualifications, rather than, or as much as, by the quality of their writing and arguments.

Insight

The enormous expansion of the higher education system has tended to result in a great deal of the intellectual life of countries taking place through the medium of universities. It is less easy for an intellectual to have a life that is separated from the university system. The disadvantage of this is that the norms and conventions of the formal academic world tend to permeate intellectual work. University conventions of academic writing are, however, an ideology, and like all ideologies represent but a partial picture of the totality.

In addition, Foucault argued that some intellectuals become so specialized in terms of their subject material that they tend not to realize the wider significance of the issues on which they are commenting. They tend to lose sight of the ways in which different issues interact and relate to each other. However, on balance, Foucault felt that the great intellectual themes of social or political thought had less relevance for the postmodern age, and that what was needed was to examine issues as they actually occurred at the micro level of society. In that way the examination of processes could be done in situ and was, in that way, more relevant to research on society.

Insight

While it is a plausible argument that a postmodern society, with its many technical areas, requires specialist academics and intellectuals, simply because the subject material is so specialized, the possible drawback is that intellectual life becomes too narrow. Great emphasis is often placed, for example, upon the academic qualifications of intellectuals, and the number of academic research articles that they have written.

One of the reasons that Foucault generally did not like making sweeping generalizations about political issues or questions of political ideology was that the process compelled him to work within a particular frame of reference. He was in a sense forced to analyse issues within a particular theoretical paradigm, usually the one that was politically dominant in a certain society. Even if he produced a critique of a particular organization or administration, the defence and subsequent discussion remained within the context of the original perspective. In other words, there was no radical transformation of the original perspective, merely a discussion about its positive and negative features.

This was part of the reason why Foucault did not subscribe to the notion of the intellectual as the omniscient thinker, or what he termed the 'master of truth and justice' (Gordon, *Michel Foucault: Power/Knowledge*, p. 126). He preferred to keep open all avenues of enquiry in order that possible solutions to problems were not obscured. In a way, one might argue that this approach is more in keeping with the true spirit of scientific endeavour because it keeps open the potential for looking at an issue or problem in different ways, rather than adopting a closed approach to a problem. According to Foucault, 'the role of an intellectual is not to tell others what they have to do' (Kritzman, *Michel Foucault: Politics, Philosophy, Culture*, p. 265).

Foucault thought that there was sometimes a tendency for people to adopt very firm and rigid ideological positions with regard to problems. The difficulty with this was, according to Foucault, that, if someone made a suggestion based largely, but perhaps not exclusively, upon a particular ideological position, it would be criticized predominantly from the alternative ideological position. Foucault preferred to be able to take each and every argument solely upon its merits, and to evaluate it as such. He preferred to keep an open rather than a closed mind, and to consider all the different sides of issues.

In any case, as Foucault argued, ideologies do not remain constant. They fluctuate throughout history, adapting to different social and political circumstances. Therefore, to argue from an exclusively ideological position seemed to Foucault to be rather inflexible. It constrained one's ideas so that it was difficult to totally address the different elements of a situation.

Foucault did not appear to support notions of **a-priori** truth in the world. Rather he was an empirical sociologist. He did not accept the idea of large-scale, sweeping truths that appeared to encircle all facets of society. He did, however, view society as an extremely complex network of social relations in which ideas were continually being defined and redefined. Such a perception removed the need for ideologies and fixed systems of thought, because the nature of truth was perceived as a varying entity, subject to new ideas and insights.

The idea of the intellectual who sits in an ivory tower and analyses society and its problems in an a priori fashion was anathema to

Foucault. 'Academic' and 'book' knowledge was inadequate as far as he was concerned in understanding society. Such knowledge had to be related to the practicalities of real issues, before it could contribute something tangible to an understanding of societal problems.

The 'specific' intellectual

We have noted that Foucault did not align himself with the concept of the 'universal' intellectual, or person who adopted the role of pronouncing upon all the key issues of the day, and of suggesting the appropriate directions in which society ought to move. Instead, he preferred the role of the 'specific' intellectual, or person who restricted himself or herself to more focused, specialized issues. However, once Foucault had attained a degree of fame it became more and more difficult for him to avoid the role of the wide-ranging thinker. People looked to him to comment upon many different issues, and almost imperceptibly he arguably began to move towards the role of the universal intellectual that he preferred in principle to avoid.

Insight

Although Foucault was, in effect, placed in a position where he was asked to comment on a diversity of issues, he still tended to avoid pronouncing on these from the perspective of a specific ideology. He thus tried to retain the flexibility of looking at questions from different viewpoints.

Foucault always sought to point out that he did not particularly wish to try to alter the political views of others. He had no specific ambition to mould the political nature of society or to encourage others to formulate political policy. Nevertheless, he did still wish to change society but in a rather different way. He perceived his role as an intellectual as being to change the way in which people thought about concepts, problems and the nature of our understanding about society. He wished therefore to show people how they did not need to take issues in society for granted, or to have to accept the existing paradigms within which people normally thought. He wanted to demonstrate how existing paradigms could be challenged, and how individuals could alter the conceptual boundaries that limited the way in which they thought. He did not want people to stay with the same assumptions or to remain with the traditional viewpoints that they had inherited. Through his writing, Foucault also wanted to demonstrate to others the ways in which he went about analysing the issues that were important to him. In a sense, he hoped to teach by example.

For Foucault, the ultimate means of analysing society was the use of rationality and logic, applied to the complexities of society. Although Foucault had studied some philosophy, he did not regard himself as essentially a philosopher. Nevertheless, he considered it important that those who communicated through the mass media did so by means of a style of academic writing and analysis that was typical of intellectuals.

Truth and the intellectual

Foucault's analysis of truth and its origins is very much linked to his conception of the intellectual. Foucault's discussion of the nature of truth was that of a relativist rather than an absolutist. He did not hold the notion of truth as a priori, independent of the empirical nature of the world. Rather he saw truth as being created by the social milieu, and conditions of the particular society in which we find ourselves. In a different society the nature of the 'truth' would be different depending upon the empirical conditions of that environment. Each society, according to Foucault's view, develops a conception of truth that is determined variously by the economic forces that are prevalent in that society, the political and ideological influences that prevail, and the historical factors that have combined to create the nature of the contemporary society. Philosophy is, according to Foucault, 'the problematization of a present' (Kritzman, *Michel Foucault: Politics, Philosophy, Culture*, p. 88). Depending upon the conditions in the society, a variety of other factors may also be influential. According to Foucault's argument, it follows therefore that in a world of diversity of truth, it is not possible to be an intellectual or thinker whose analysis can range far and wide across this range of ideas. One can only specialize and comment upon a particular narrow area of human academic activity. In other words, one can only be a specific intellectual.

Insight

As education systems have expanded in postmodern societies, specialist knowledge has increasingly become located in universities. Vocational knowledge, once maintained outside the university system, is now increasingly located within it, and universities have diversified enormously in the subjects offered in degree programmes. This diversification also applies to research, which is now conducted in a much wider range of fields than was previously the case.

Foucault was, however, somewhat sceptical of the function of intellectuals as he saw them as to some extent agents of the power base of the state. As intellectuals are to be increasingly identified as existing within universities, and as the latter are to a large extent funded by the state, it is difficult to imagine intellectuals as being totally separate from state authority. We may speak of academic independence, and of the autonomy of the intellectual, but the economic arrangements between academic institutions and state finance would appear to some extent at least to erode the independence of academic spirit. Governments, for example, are major sponsors of research studentships and of primary research. Through these means, the state has an influence over the nature of the research conducted in universities, encouraging one area of enquiry, and making it more difficult for another area to be pursued.

Insight

One might argue that there is a danger of creating a kind of intellectual monopoly within the university system. The expansion of the higher education system may make it more and more difficult for intellectuals to be accepted if they are not affiliated to a university in some way.

Each epoch had, for Foucault, a different mode of thinking that was particularly characterized by a mode of linguistic communication. At different points in the historical development of culture, different forms of discourse became dominant, depending at least in part upon prevalent features of society at the time. The modern period of development, typified especially by a rapidly expanding industrial environment, modelled on a capitalist economic system, produced a context in which, according to Foucault, the universal intellectual could flourish. The essential nature of the relationship between owner of capital and the means of production, and those who sold their labour, was one of conflict. These social classes were set in opposition to each other. In such a situation, the proletariat, overworked, exploited, deprived of the capacity for self-determination, and often, most importantly, unaware of the nature of their true economic and political position, required writers with broad-based understanding who were able to help the working classes comprehend the true nature of economic relations in society. Foucault argued that such writers and intellectuals who operated within such a sweeping perspective were both needed by, and characteristic of, such a political system.

However, as society became transformed into postmodernity, with entirely different economic relationships, and a different technological base, the need became evident for a different type of intellectual. The increasingly specialized nature of technology, for example, required scientists and engineers who were capable of understanding and communicating within extremely narrow fields of expertise. It was simply no longer realistic to expect one writer to encompass the entire range of human endeavour. In previous times it had been possible for the liberally minded 'man of letters' to comment upon such diverse fields as literature, history, mathematics and science, but this was no longer realistic. So specialized have fields of endeavour become that it can be extremely difficult for researchers in different areas of science to communicate with each other, quite apart from, say, an art historian communicating with a molecular biologist.

In addition, specific intellectuals approach the analysis of research problems in very different ways. Consider the case of two art historians discussing the significance of a painting in the development of a period of art. They may not agree on each other's point of view, but they will probably share the same type of concepts, the same criteria by which to judge paintings, and the same type of discourse within which to communicate. They will in effect share the same approach to determining the legitimacy or otherwise of a judgement about a painting. In a very different way, the researcher or intellectual operating in the field of molecular biology will adopt a very different range of procedures and ways of approaching an investigation. The biologist and the art historian would probably find it very difficult to adopt each other's techniques for their own research enquiries.

Insight

Although in principle it may be very difficult for those in the sciences and in the humanities to maintain effective communication, it is possible for research in one area to help that in another. For example, different kinds of scientific dating procedures may be very useful in determining the age of works of art.

One of the problems of the specific intellectual stems from the increased specialization which they are almost forced to undertake. Whereas the universal intellectual was able to communicate on various themes with a wide range of the general public, the specific intellectual finds this rather difficult since he or she is versed only in a very narrow specialism.

Foucault was a great advocate of the intellectual being completely honest and saying exactly what he or she thought in a situation. Sometimes this might entail a degree of danger to the intellectual, depending upon the issue, but Foucault felt that the notion of speaking frankly about issues was very much a part of the idea of being an intellectual. Very often it happens that the intellectual does not possess any power, in terms of political and economic power, and only has the force of his own words at his disposal.

On the other hand, those who hold opposing views to the intellectual, or who represent various institutions or vested interests, may be considerably more powerful, and may be in a position to mount considerable opposition to the intellectual. In such situations, it may take considerable courage on the part of the intellectual to oppose such vested interests by speaking out.

Insight

It is often the case that in times of social injustice, society looks to the intellectual to speak out in order to try to change things. This often places the intellectual in a difficult position, and considerable personal courage is often required to challenge the authority of those in power.

Sometimes it may be that the intellectual is speaking to, or writing something destined for, a group of people who are strongly associated with an opposing viewpoint. They may have devoted time and energy, and even money, to supporting this alternative viewpoint, and may be quite firmly determined to oppose the views of the intellectual. The intellectual is thus often confronted by an ethical dilemma: whether to speak out and incur the displeasure of the powerful, or to maintain silence and thus align himself or herself with those in authority. Foucault considered that the act of truth-telling and of being outspoken, no matter how dangerous this might be to the intellectual, becomes a form of moral duty that cannot be avoided. If one purports to be an intellectual, then openness and honesty in speech are almost necessary requirements. Foucault noted, however, that it was increasingly difficult for the specific intellectual to challenge the entrenched powers of the state or the great institutions because they simply did not possess the breadth of vision that would enable them to do this. The day of the universal intellectual who could challenge the great authorities of the land appeared to be over, and one gains the impression, rightly or wrongly, that Foucault regretted the passing of such figures.

Foucault, however, appears not to be pessimistic about the future. He is open to the notion that there are enormous advances to be made in human knowledge, and that intellectuals are the people who will achieve this advance. Nevertheless, Foucault feels that there are considerable inadequacies in the way in which the academic establishments work, and the way in which specific intellectuals tackle the problem of achieving advances in knowledge.

Foucault found it very interesting that, with the decline of Sartrean existentialism as the key school of philosophical thought in France, there seemed not to be a replacement. Foucault was in fact apparently quite pleased about this because he felt that one dominant school of thought would have an adverse effect on free philosophical thought. In fact, Foucault, like Jean-François Lyotard, felt that it was simply not possible to identify one school of thought that was capable of meeting the diverse demands of contemporary society. In its place, Foucault was pleased to note that what had developed in postmodernity was not a universal school of any particular philosophy, but rather a philosophy devoted to methods of transforming society. This was not a philosophy that purported to provide various overarching or meta-analyses of society, but rather a philosophy that sought to give individual people the mechanisms for examining and transforming society.

Insight

One might argue that this idea was more empowering for ordinary people. It made them much less dependent on what might be termed the 'great intellects' of the age, and encouraged them to be much more autonomous and self-reflective, finding their own solutions to the major problems and issues of the time.

Foucault was also in some ways rather anti-intellectual in the sense that he was concerned that, throughout the history of the analysis of culture, the latter has largely been interpreted through the means of the discussion of literature. In other words, the culture of a society at a particular period has been interpreted, argued Foucault, by an interpretation of the most scholarly, academic literature available. Now, as Foucault pointed out, this type of literature is not the only type produced in a society at a given time, and indeed may not normally be in the majority in terms of the total literary output. It may therefore be more representative, as Foucault pointed out, to analyse the totality of literary production from a society, rather than concentrating on only the scholarly literature produced by the intellectual community. It could be argued that this would be the most democratic approach to the study of culture and literature.

Insight

Some may argue that within a particular society there are examples of culture (what we may term 'high culture') that are in effect more valuable or more profound in their style or ideas, and hence deserving of more study and reflection. It may therefore be argued that other forms of culture are implicitly less valuable or worthy. On the other hand, one might take a more democratic view and consider all manifestations of culture to be different but having the same intrinsic worth.

The intellectual and culture

Foucault also spoke of the role of the intellectual as a critic of culture – of plays, novels, poetry, music and art. He did not, however, favour the act of purely analysing and critiquing art and culture, but preferred the intellectual in the capacity of someone who encourages and stimulates the creative impulse in others. Foucault saw the intellectual as a mentor, someone who would help younger, creative people to transform their ideas into reality. He found this to be a much more positive and human role for an intellectual, rather than merely acting as a critic, however intelligent and penetrating his or her insights.

Insight

One could argue that the role of critic implies that the intellectual possesses rather special abilities to distinguish between forms of culture of different worth. The intellectual

as mentor, however, suggests a much more supportive
role – one in which the intellectual does not make value
judgements about culture.

Foucault noted a considerable disjuncture between the critic and
the writer. Critics perhaps feel that they can make no remark at
all without people feeling that they are being too negative. From
their point of view, critics probably feel that they are generating
useful insights into a piece of creative work, and incidentally
helping others to understand it, and perhaps in addition assisting
in marketing and publicizing a book. Writers, on the other hand,
probably feel that they are subject to excessive and undue criticism
from critics.

Intellectuals who act sometimes as critics and analysts of literature
probably feel also that they need to identify significant issues
to write about. From the writer's view, the problem with this
requirement to identify major issues upon which to comment is
that the analysis may evolve into criticism for its own sake.

Although Foucault is often described as being in total opposition
to the existentialist Sartre, one can discern the possibility of
similarities between them. Just as Sartre was influenced by a
Marxist humanism, one can identify in Foucault a strong empathy
for the dispossessed, the disenfranchised, and those in general,
who for any reason, are unable to assert their rights in society.
However, the differences between Foucault and Sartre became
much more evident when one considers the primacy of the
individual human subject in the philosophy of Sartre, as opposed
to the emphasis in Foucault's work of the way in which institutions
and organizations influence the nature of knowledge through
the exercise of power relations. All the same, Foucault was never
entirely persuaded that the role of the individual was no longer
relevant to society. There was, he had to occasionally concede,
a need for the universal intellectual to guide the individual in
challenging the major institutions of society. There were certainly
many areas in which Foucault challenged the political and social
status quo of society, and in so doing demonstrated many of the

characteristics of the engaged, left-wing, revolutionary intellectual as personified by Sartre.

Foucault never stinted in his acknowledgement of the contribution of Sartre to the political and moral climate of France in the period after World War II. Foucault accepted that Sartre had done a great deal as an intellectual to make the wider French public aware of the great issues of the time, and to ensure that these analyses were not simply restricted to academics in higher education and to other intellectuals. After the events of 1968, Sartre and Foucault were both interested in ways of conceptualizing the position of students and workers in France, and in the wider Europe. They both accepted in a sense that, in an increasingly postmodern world, it was necessary to address the disenchantment of society in the face of large-scale and entrenched organizations and the accompanying bureaucracy.

Although there would appear to be far more in common between Sartre and Foucault than is commonly accepted, Foucault retained a certain suspicion throughout his career about the independence of the individual. Foucault viewed the individual as inevitably distorted by socialization, and by the general societal influences that are brought to bear. However, this was perhaps less of a problem for Sartre, who accepted the essential subjectivity of the individual, and that the latter would be inevitably affected by personal and developmental factors.

10 THINGS TO REMEMBER

1 *The 'universal' intellectual was typically someone who passed judgement on the major issues of the day, and to whom people looked for guiding advice on significant moral and political questions.*

2 *Foucault noted that traditionally it had been the writer and author who typified the role of the universal intellectual.*

3 *Society often expected the intellectual to be the one to speak out at times of oppression, or when human rights were being infringed.*

4 *In the postmodern age, Foucault felt that the role of the intellectual demanded someone who had a more specialized knowledge of issues, someone who could be termed a 'specific' rather than 'universal' intellectual.*

5 *Foucault considered that one of the difficulties with specific intellectuals was that, because of their specialized interests, it was arguably more difficult for them to see some of the linkages between issues.*

6 *In the postmodern world, intellectuals are often linked to the university system, with the attendant risk that they are all operating within a particular kind of educational ideology.*

7 *As ideologies change and adapt throughout history, Foucault felt that it was unduly restrictive to keep to a single ideological position when analysing issues.*

8 *Foucault argued that he had no wish per se to alter the political views of people, but tried, on the other hand, to encourage people to think about issues in an open-minded and critical way.*

(Contd)

9 *Foucault did not hold the view that there were absolute truths in the world, but rather that all questions should be open to empirical enquiry.*

10 *Foucault was less in favour of the intellectual who acted as a critic in the arts and literature; he preferred the intellectual to act as mentor, supporting the creative activity in younger artists and writers.*

10

Retrospect of a life

In this chapter you will review:
- *some aspects of the life of Michel Foucault*
- *some of the key features of his writing and research*
- *his ideas concerning the mechanisms of power.*

The approach of Foucault

It is now more than a quarter of a century since the death of Michel Foucault, and yet he still remains an emblematic figure. His shaven head, and rather monastic appearance that was somewhat at odds perhaps with the realities of his life, make him immediately recognizable. The subject matter of his research and writing was, in addition, somewhat unusual. He sought out, in historical sources, extreme and unusual cases in order to use them to explicate partly the contemporary world order, but also the way in which our knowledge of the world was affected by our manner of discussing events. His capacity to shock both the general public and an academic audience by reference to these extreme instances may well be a factor in the continued interest in his writing and analyses of society. Foucault was also resolute in his determination to avoid, absolutely, being categorized or labelled as a certain type of intellectual or academic. It would have been easy for him to attach himself to a particular school of thought within philosophy or psychology, but he perceived this as a potential infringement of his liberty. He was to guard this independence of spirit throughout his life. Perhaps this also explains something of the continued interest in his ideas. Schools of philosophy come and go, along with those who are ideologically attached to them. In addition, his openness to different ideas within philosophy and history results in his having a wide audience. The act of belonging to a narrow school of thought can be very restricting, limited only to those who share that particular ideology.

Insight

It is difficult to imagine Foucault ever becoming unfashionable in academic circles. The diversity of his writing means that he is very difficult to place in a particular school of thought, and hence he is relatively immune from attempts to categorize him.

Foucault was also somewhat unconventional in his private life, breaking the boundaries of the stereotypical lifestyle of the university academic. Perhaps this broadened his public and gave him an audience beyond that of the usual run of attendees at scholarly conferences and readers of articles in academic journals. He was also an advocate of many different political and social causes, largely characterized perhaps by an attempt to argue for the poor, the dispossessed, the oppressed and those who found it rather difficult to present their own case to those in power. This often meant that he was, like Sartre, a supporter of left-wing causes. However, it sometimes resulted in his support for causes that were perhaps less popular in Europe, such as the religiously inspired revolution in Iran. Nevertheless, there was a definite consistency in his defence of those groups or classes in society that appeared to be treated disadvantageously by powerful institutions and organizations. Foucault also exhibited a good deal of personal courage, particularly in the course of political demonstrations. He was never afraid to be at the forefront of confrontation, and in personal risk of danger. Finally in a sense he combined the polarities of the French academic milieu: on the one hand, as a professor at Vincennes, standing shoulder to shoulder with the radical, militant, left-wing students, he represented the epitome of social change against the intellectual establishment; and yet, on the other, as a professor at the Collège de France, he represented the elite of the French academic tradition. The sheer diversity of his work hence attracts people of widely different interests, and perhaps explains why so many students today draw inspiration from his writing. Whether in the fields of sociology, psychology, criminology, philosophy, or the history of ideas, Foucault is frequently cited by students in their essays or dissertations. His work is easily adapted and applied to many different subjects, helping to shed light on many different issues and problems.

Insight

It may be that the unconventional, unpredictable nature of Foucault's life is part of the reason he is popular with students. He is not, perhaps, seen as part of the academic establishment. Students are also able to cite his work in many different contexts, simply because he was so diverse in his work.

The nonconformist

What then is the legacy of Michel Foucault? How can we best summarize his contribution to our intellectual development and history? First of all, Foucault appears to have been, certainly from his university days in Paris, something of an iconoclast. He appears to have had rather a reputation as someone unconventional, who was a nonconformist even in the context of Parisian student life. He also developed a strong sense of affinity for those who were disadvantaged in society, and felt very firmly that those who wielded power in society should do more to help those who did not possess the resources to have a reasonable quality of life. It was this type of perspective that linked Foucault very much to the Sartrean tradition, even though he was reluctant to simply follow in the slipstream of existentialism. Perhaps one of the reasons for Foucault wishing to distance himself from Sartre was that he valued his own independence so much. He really did not wish to attach himself to one of the great philosophical systems of the twentieth century, and to thereby 'belong' to a particular school of thought. He felt that this would be far too restrictive.

> **Insight**
> Foucault, it seemed, greatly valued his own independence.
> His intermittent interest, and indeed obsession, with suicide
> suggests that he felt himself in some sense to be separate from
> the world. Neither did he appear to have any desire to fit in
> with other people's thoughts: rather he devoted himself to his
> own thoughts.

One might think of Foucault perhaps as exemplifying the characteristics of postmodern society, and in particular the notion proposed by Jean-François Lyotard, that the so-called 'meta-narratives' were no longer applicable. Although Lyotard's book on this subject was published towards the end of Foucault's life, there were already challenges to the idea of large-scale theories of society. A meta-narrative was seen by Lyotard as an all-embracing perspective on society that explained all of human existence by means of a unified world view. Lyotard argued that in the postmodern world such perspectives had become increasingly redundant, and that society had increasingly diversified, so that the postmodern intellectual was free to select from a wide range of approaches in order to understand society. This approach seems to be convergent with that of Foucault who apparently tried to avoid subscribing to a particular meta-narrative, and instead selected whichever world view or theoretical perspective seemed most appropriate or relevant at the time in order to explain phenomena. Foucault has thus left us with an approach to research, an approach to understanding the world and to generating new knowledge, that is, in a sense, *not* an approach. At least, it is not a singular perspective that purports to supply a universal understanding of the world. Rather it is a broad way of looking at research that encourages the researcher to think carefully about the purpose of the enquiry, and then to adopt whichever theoretical perspective appears to be the most relevant.

> **Insight**
> Foucault's distaste for what have been termed 'meta-narratives' may have been partly because of his fierce independence of spirit, and partly because he did not wish to follow in the footsteps of another academic.

Foucault and social construction

Foucault applied a similar method of looking at the diversity of the world to his examination and analysis of the social sciences, and in particular of psychological disciplines. There had been a tendency, derived in some part from the **positivist** perspective in sociology, to view the social sciences as linked together by a range of concepts that could be applied in a variety of different situations. In other words, they were absolutist concepts that did not depend upon their context for their meaning. Foucault challenged this idea, which could be linked to the notion of meta-narratives. What he argued was that such sociological and psychological concepts were not absolute, a priori, ideas, but were a social construction derived from the economic, social, philosophical, political and historical contexts of the period. Such concepts were a social creation. Not only that, but the nature of these concepts evolved and changed with society, and were characteristic of a particular mode of thinking or discourse.

Insight

Foucault can be said to belong to what is termed the 'sociology of knowledge' perspective. He argued that knowledge is constructed through the process of interaction between human beings, during which reality is negotiated, and may evolve through the process of further discussions. Within this perspective, knowledge is relative rather than absolute because it is produced through interpersonal discourse.

From this analysis of social science concepts as essentially relativist emerged Foucault's critique of, for example, the definition and treatment of those classified as 'insane' or 'mad'. Foucault criticized the contemporary model of 'madness' as requiring the use of medication to alter the brain's chemistry, or of surgical or other intervention such as electric shock therapy, as reflecting a particular social definition of madness that was not necessarily valid. To put Foucault's argument another way, such therapies and approaches were not necessarily 'scientific', according to Foucault, but merely reflected the ideology of the period that perceived such 'medical' treatment as the valid approach. In other words, Foucault was pleading for a different way of thinking about the knowledge that was defined as acceptable at a particular time in historical development. He was arguing that we should not be placidly convinced that, just because a particular mode of looking at the world, or of gaining knowledge about the world, was regarded as the definitive approach, we should assume it is acceptable. On the contrary, we should learn to challenge the **epistemological** status quo, and should ask questions about the validity of the accepted mode of scientific thinking.

The same type of arguments can be applied to other branches of medicine and science. It could be argued that in a postmodern society we have a particular conception of medical treatment that involves the extensive use of drugs on the one hand, and the use of surgical intervention, on the other. We tend to accept the ideology of 'scientific' diagnosis, followed by the specific localized treatment of a malfunctioning area. There are, however, an increasing number of alternatives to this approach, variously labelled holistic medicine and herbal medicine, and also the use of acupuncture, and various ancient therapies such as ayurvedic medicine. In other words, Foucault has reminded us of a very important dimension of life. We should not necessarily become committed to a particular way of thinking about the world, simply because it is the prevalent ideology or is the accepted truth. We should be willing to consider other approaches and think perhaps of looking at the world in a different way.

Insight

Foucault was in favour of our being prepared to consider new approaches to problems, and not to automatically use the traditional method. We should, he felt, be questioning, and sceptical, in the true tradition of the scientific method.

Equally, perhaps, we can reflect upon the proposition that we live in a world in which the prevalent paradigm is the scientific method of thinking. Although this particular paradigm has brought enormous advances for humanity, and the capacity to at least partially control the world through technology, it may not necessarily be the final word on the means by which the human race may continue to exist and evolve. In the field of parapsychology, for example, we have a wide range of empirical observations that are not explainable within the parameters of contemporary science. It may be that at the very least, the scientific paradigm should be revised in order to incorporate these observations. There is also the world of spiritual experience, of religion and of faith. These experiences are extremely meaningful to many millions of people, and it is not beyond the limits of reasonableness that within the world of the spirit rests another paradigm that has enormous potential for the development of humanity.

Insight

It was quite possible, according to Foucault, that the prevalent perspective of a particular period could relatively easily be replaced by another. In other words, we may be familiar with a particular approach to problem-solving, but that does not mean that it is automatically the most appropriate method to employ.

Foucault was particularly interested in the history of punishment, and the way in which contemporary systems of punishment did not focus upon the harsh physical punishment of the individual, but upon a system of observation, of ensuring that individual citizens behaved according to certain norms accepted within society, and of controlling behaviour until those norms were attained. Foucault was absolutely correct in his analysis of the significance of observation for postmodern society. We have become very familiar with the power of the state to observe its citizens in many different locations, ranging from the centre of cities to motorways and a variety of organizations such as banks, libraries and shops. Advances in satellite and camera technology mean that the individual can be video-recorded on many different occasions during each day. Motorists, in particular, are only too aware of the way in which their driving patterns can be effectively monitored without their seeing or coming into contact with police. Many aspects of our behaviour can be easily monitored by computers.

These include such diverse activities as our borrowing patterns at a library, our use of certain Internet websites, our retail shopping habits, and our patterns of overseas travel. This information can then be employed to judge whether we are complying with either legal requirements, or simply with norms of acceptable behaviour.

The state and the individual

Foucault maintained a strong interest in the manner in which the state ensured that individual citizens complied with the demands of the government. He was interested in the methods employed by the state, and the strategies that were developed to manipulate the behaviour of citizens. Much depends upon the way in which we view these issues. We can, on the one hand, perceive such measures as malevolent, and very controlling of the individual. We can see these methods as an assault upon our autonomy, and sense of self-determination. On the other hand, one might argue that, in a complex postmodern society, it is essential for the state to manage and control individuals in order that society can function much more effectively.

Insight

The ability to observe citizens and hence exert social control is an important feature of contemporary society, argued Foucault. Later technology, including the widespread use of mobile phones, has enabled the state to know the exact location of citizens at any time.

There is an important contemporary debate that focuses upon this very dilemma highlighted by Foucault. Analysts note an increasing tendency for the state to interest itself in aspects of our lives that were previously hidden from view. Previously, the nature of the food we eat, and the amount of food consumed, was not considered a legitimate topic of concern for government. However, as government begins to argue that there exists correlations between obesity and illness, and also between the types of food consumed and, for example, vascular disease, the state begins to want to control far more what we consume. The argument of the state is that, as it is required to provide health services for the citizen, then it has a right to try to encourage healthy eating. Other areas in which the state is beginning to concern itself include the manner in which adults conduct their role as a parent; the amount of exercise people take; the way in which they consume energy either in motor vehicles or in the insulation of their homes, and the extent to which they consume alcohol. It would probably not surprise Foucault that there is an increasing tendency for government to interest itself in such matters, and from time to time to legislate on these questions. On the other hand, there is an ethical debate to be had about the degree to which such state intervention is desirable, and the extent to which it represents an unacceptable erosion of human liberty and autonomy. Foucault argued that all of these strategies of observation and recording of, and intervention in, what some may view as the private lives of citizens represents the exercise of power by the state over its citizenry. In terms of surveillance, it is interesting that individuals do not know whether or not they are being observed, but the omnipresence of cameras emphasizes to the individual that there is always the potential for them to be observed. This potential is often sufficient to cause people to amend their behaviour, and to comply with the accepted norms of the state.

Insight

As we are observed more and more, there are serious ethical questions about whether it is reasonable to continue such detailed observation of people, or whether it infringes their personal liberty. One facet of the question is whether the information so obtained is, or can be, used for specific legitimate reasons, or whether it is simply collected for potential use in the future.

In his general arguments about the extension of state power over the individual, Foucault also argued that the state was concerning itself more and more with a biological and medical control of the individual. He further argued that this was less about caring for the health and medical condition of the individuals, but more about the subtle and gradual exercise of power over the individual. Foucault argued that, above all else, the state had to ensure the control of its citizens, and that this was one of its major strategies in doing so. There is a need, for example, for the supply of donor organs, and states are beginning to encourage people to make their organs available for transplant on their death. Equally, there is an ongoing debate about voluntary euthanasia. Opponents of this are concerned with at least one scenario, by which individuals might in the future, at times of scarce medical resources, be 'encouraged' to accept euthanasia because it is difficult for the authorities to sustain treatment. We are all aware of the difficulties of funding a national health system, and it is not difficult to gaze into the future and to imagine practical instances of the developments envisaged by Foucault, and the consequences for the power capable of being exercised by the state.

Foucault was, in general, very concerned about the ideology of the exercise of power being justified on the grounds purely of sustaining the health and welfare of the populace. The reason he was concerned about this was that he felt it was an ideology that was very easy to support, and very plausible as far as the population was concerned. Moreover, using this ideology as a means of persuasion, it would become possible for the state to argue for a wide range of political measures. Foucault was interested in the complex of methods employed by the state to gain and sustain power over the population.

There is an illuminating comparison here with the approach of Karl Marx. It is understandable that Marx, living through the period of the industrial revolution, and the advent of the modern era, saw the context of industrial and technological production as being the locus of power in society. Those who owned the factories, and controlled both the distribution of labour and the creation of goods, controlled also the creation of wealth. With this went power. Those who exercised control over the production process had access to economic power and also political power. With the transition from a modern society founded upon industrial production, to a postmodern society founded upon technological knowledge, the nature and context of power became different. In a postmodern society, the emphasis evolved into the acquisition of sophisticated, technological knowledge that was increasingly stored and disseminated by means of computers. The emphasis developed into the capacity to communicate and transfer complex knowledge. Although power was certainly associated with knowledge transfer, it was by no means as localized as in a modern society. In a modern society, the individual with the most power was the person who owned the factory. In a postmodern society, the nature of power was much more diffuse. Complicated networks of communication connected different loci of technology and of power, and the nature of the latter appeared to often be moving. The world as envisaged by Foucault often seems very uncertain. It is difficult to identify the location of power and authority in society, and it is also difficult to discern a clear sequence of events in social and political history. This uncertainty may be disconcerting, but it may also represent a truer metaphor for society than a model in which we can find more reassuring certainty. Previous models of historical development tended to try to present a logical sequence of events and developments, each affected to some extent by the former. In Foucault's vision, however, historical development is much more uncertain, a network of developments, sometimes advancing and sometimes receding. It is sometimes difficult to discern a series of developments moved forwards by a chain of causation. The prevalent historical forces seem vague and ill-defined, leading to a network of power relations in which no single person or entity appears to be in control.

One can appreciate why Foucault did not wish to provide an all-encompassing account of history, but nevertheless this absence of a general theory does make it rather difficult sometimes to both understand his ideas, and to apply them to different contexts. Foucault's methodology tended to be to identify interesting case studies, and then to proceed to extract as much data as possible, subsequently generalizing to other situations. In terms of research design, however, he does not appear to have adopted a systematic selection of cases, which could have been used to generate a theory, but to have employed a certain degree of serendipity in his study of particular instances. In his studies of contemporary phenomena there is often room for far more empirical data that would assist in the generation of theoretical concepts, or at least in the elucidation of new concepts. The origin of the theoretical concepts employed in Foucault's research is not always clear. Normally, theoretical concepts are either borrowed or adapted from previous research, or are developed from empirical observations using a grounded theory approach. In Foucault's research, however, the theoretical concepts that he employs in his work often appear to have been developed almost intuitively, rather than having been derived systematically from an empirical source. This can lead to an uncertainty and lack of clarity in what he is arguing.

Methodology and research

Foucault's essential difficulty is that he resisted all possibility of using conventional methodologies within sociology or psychology. If he were, for example, to develop a theory that was founded upon, say, an ethnographic approach or a phenomenological research methodology, then he was afraid that he would become the sort of universal model or intellectual that filled him with unease. Not only did he not want to become the disciple of a universal intellectual, but neither did he wish to become such a person himself. He felt that if he were to succumb to such a role, then he would automatically have the kind of power and authority over others that he abhorred. Foucault tended to view the exercise of power as a sort of game in which different sources of power and authority vied for control over the others. To Foucault this was not in a sense something that he needed to demonstrate, but was a phenomenon that was readily visible for those who cared to reflect carefully enough about the social circumstances around them. To that extent, Foucault was in a sense arguing for the use of analytic philosophy, in which one did not try to determine certain types of truth through empirical means, but recognized that there were forms of knowledge that were capable of being validated and determined by analysing the very concepts used to describe them.

Throughout his studies of historical development, Foucault was interested in the mechanisms whereby subjects developed and evolved. The usual model posited was a linear one in which one approach to a subject had various consequences for another variant of the subject, and thus a particular discipline evolved. There was thus a cause-and-effect model. Foucault found this explanation overly simplistic, and one that did not account for the power relations that existed within the mechanisms for the development of knowledge. This system presupposed that those able to influence the development of knowledge through the political or economic power that they wielded would be able, within a linear model, to influence the way in which knowledge developed in the future. Foucault, however, supposed that the development of knowledge progressed in much more of a matrix fashion. In order to truly comprehend changes in knowledge, one needed to search for the *network* of changes that were taking place in context at the time. The linear model, according to Foucault, was simply not sufficiently sophisticated to explain epistemological changes in different societies.

Foucault applied the same conceptual argument to the notion of the workings of democracy. He pointed out that, although there was the assumption that an elected government exercised power on behalf of the electorate, this was a far too simplistic notion. Foucault argued that, in reality, power was far more dispersed than this model might suggest. In fact, power was distributed throughout society, and primarily it was located within institutions that had no democratic accountability to the electorate. The functioning of a state ultimately depended on the ways in which such institutions collaborated and interacted in order to help the state function. Foucault did not appear to be arguing that *all* power was distributed in this dispersed network, but that in the past social scientists and historians had not taken sufficient notice of this mechanism in society. However, notwithstanding the insights of Foucault's approach, it is also important to recognize that focusing upon the micro aspects of society makes it more difficult to generalize about society and to formulate general laws. Ultimately, in order to make sense of society, and to employ that understanding in generating policy decisions, one needs to take account of the more general loci of power – the great institutions and indeed the state itself.

There is thus a tension between macro, institutional power and the micro, dispersed power that is close to the individual and that tries to ensure that the individual becomes adapted and socialized to the norms of society. This process of socialization is reinforced by numerous mechanisms, but in particular by procedures of observation. Foucault was very conscious, however, that learning to comply with social norms sometimes results in an uncritical adherence to the status quo in society.

Perhaps for this reason, Foucault tended from time to time to lend his support towards movements and groups that were trying to change society, and to introduce new political and economic systems. The clearest example would be during the student unrest of 1968, but also in his work to publicize the conditions of prisoners. Interestingly, though, the motivation for this challenge to society was not a humanitarian morality based upon the notion of improving conditions for the subjective individual. For Foucault the individual person, who had been at the focus of the existentialism of Sartre, was not the prime concern. Foucault was much more interested in examining the nature of the relationship between individuals and the loci of power, and of transforming those relationships. In doing so, however, Foucault did not in any way support the notion of an ideology that purported to explain all the phenomena in the social world. In other words, an ideology such as Marxism, or alternatively free-market capitalism, were anathema to him. He felt that, in their different ways, such ideologies exerted an oppressive power over people.

Ideology and power

Ideologies need not necessarily be political or economic, according to Foucault; they could also be philosophical. He did not support, for example, the philosophical rationalism of the modern period.

While acknowledging that rational thought, and the rational scientific process, brought technological advances, it was for Foucault a separate question whether this resulted in a better quality of life for human beings. It is easy to assume that advances in knowledge and new discoveries in science, even in social science, can take place independently and objectively, without any consideration of the power relations in society. Yet each society, through the prevalent mechanisms of power in that society, defines and controls the types of statement, the discourse, the ways of thinking and articulating ideas that are characteristic of that society. Hence it is impossible in practical terms to separate issues concerning the nature of power from issues concerning the development and validation of new knowledge and understandings. Part of the reason for this is that Foucault did not conceive of power as a quality that was possessed or owned by people. Although we talk about powerful people or less powerful people, Foucault claimed that this was not because they actually possessed more or less of this substance or quality called power. He regarded power as a process of interaction within society. Certainly some people were perhaps more skilled at using and exercising power than others, but power was not actually a commodity to be gained and then owned. In any case, there was not, according to Foucault, a fixed 'person' who could own the power. Human beings did not possess an intrinsic self according to Foucault. The person who we are is much more variable and flexible, not a fixed, rigid entity. We are so flexible because we become who we are through our interactions with other people, and these interactions are continually changing and developing.

Foucault pointed out to us that power, too, is a very flexible and variable entity. Some people who may think that they are completely powerless in society may in fact be able, under certain circumstances, to exercise considerable power. Mahatma Gandhi and his followers are a very good example of this. When the British in India placed a tax on salt, a product needed in a hot climate by the majority of the Indian population, Gandhi led some of his followers on a celebrated protest march to the coast, where salt deposits collected naturally on the sand through evaporation. People could freely collect their own salt. This greatly irritated the colonial administration, who realized that, by a very simple, non-violent means, Gandhi had managed to subvert their new tax policy. Hence, ordinary peasant farmers suddenly discovered the capacity for exercising political power. In a similar example, the British started to import into India cotton spun in the mills of Lancashire and forced the Indians to buy the cotton at inflated prices. Gandhi decided to encourage all Indians to spin their own cotton on small, hand-turned spinning wheels, and then to weave their own cloth in their homes. Again, the policy of the British colonial government was subverted by the simple expedient of self-help. Naturally, this simple measure angered the colonial administrators. In other words, given appropriate circumstances, power can be exercised by people in unusual and unexpected ways.

Foucault wished to try to examine in detail the mechanisms of power that existed in the world. He operated from the position that many of these mechanisms were obscure, difficult to identify and difficult to analyse. It is perhaps for this reason that he often employed the method of exploring individual case studies, using sometimes rare and complicated archival material. As Foucault specifically did not attach himself to a particular school of thought or to a particular research methodology, he tended not to employ a clearly circumscribed set of concepts when it came to academic research. He argued that, when he was writing, or conducting academic work, he had no particular preconceptions about how the issues would evolve. Indeed, he appeared to be arguing that when he was writing, he actually wanted to learn himself from the process of writing. This is rather similar to the concept of reflexivity in social research. Reflexivity as a concept points out that there is a continuous interaction and mutual influence between the researcher and those who are the respondents in the research. Both parties learn from each other, and inform the issue or problem being investigated.

This process of learning was central to Foucault's approach. In his historical studies he professed himself less concerned with analysing and describing the broad patterns of historical development, and more with noting the significant points of change in history. He tried to examine in detail, not only the points of transition, where one approach to society was transformed into a different perspective, but also the mechanisms that supported such transitions. He wished to examine the ways in which society changed, rather than the ways in which society continued within the same perspective. In the transition from a medieval society to a modern society, Foucault noted the increase in the need for maintaining accurate records of citizens. Whether it was in the field of employment, health, education, or indeed the judicial and penal systems, it became more and more necessary to keep accurate records of the lives of people. One of the functions of observation, allied with record-keeping, was to ensure that individuals complied with the norms decreed by society as evidence of acceptable behaviour. An increasing number of clerks and bureaucrats within society maintained this data.

In seeking to comprehend the ways in which society became transformed from one paradigm to another, it is worth noting that Foucault did not generally try to systematize the functioning of the social world. He was not interested in a reductionist approach whereby he might draw up a system of social 'rules' or 'procedures' that were typical of a society in a state of flux. In fact, if anything, he wanted to illuminate the complexities of the process of change – to show that the transition process was more complex rather than less complex.

In reflecting finally on the heritage of Foucault, it is interesting to consider the relative virtues of those thinkers who try to explain the world in terms of broad sweeping concepts, and those who, like Foucault, argue that this is too simplistic, and ultimately futile. The former approach provides us with a means to try to comprehend our surroundings and the society in which we live; while, arguably, the latter perhaps gives us a more realistic, though disconcerting idea of the workings of society and history. Which is the better? Perhaps neither. We may need both, on the grounds that the world is simply too complex to understand within a single social model or perspective. Perhaps the contribution of Michel Foucault is that he gave us an alternative vision; something to balance the sweeping schemes of the macro-theorists. That is no small gift.

10 THINGS TO REMEMBER

1 When researching, Foucault would sometimes select extreme examples of something in order to develop his academic arguments.

2 The diversity of Foucault's thought and writing, makes it difficult to place him within a particular academic school of thought.

3 At times, Foucault demonstrated considerable courage when he took part in political demonstrations.

4 Foucault was opposed to the idea of meta-narratives, feeling that more specific, localized explanations of society were more valid.

5 Foucault could be considered to belong to the sociology of knowledge perspective, whereby knowledge is created by people, through the process of interpersonal dialogue.

6 In his research, he tried a number of different methodological approaches, not adhering to simply one perspective.

7 Foucault was interested in the way in which the state employed techniques of observation in order to exercise control over its citizens.

8 He noted the complex ethical issues inherent in the use of observation on the one hand, and the related infringement of personal freedom and autonomy on the other.

9 For Foucault, power could be dispersed in society, so that groups of people who felt themselves powerless, could, under certain circumstances, be able to exercise considerable power.

10 Foucault regarded the writing of a book, not as simply the recording of predetermined knowledge, but as a personal exploration of a topic.

Glossary

A priori A priori knowledge is that which is derived, not from our senses, but from the use of pure reason. Some argue that the principles of pure mathematics or of ethics, represent a priori knowledge.

Classical Foucault described this as the historical period following the Renaissance, and characterized it by the use of scientific measurement to investigate the world around us.

Discourse Each area of social life has its own concepts and ways of communicating with them. This is referred to as discourse.

Empiricism The assertion that all knowledge is derived from data obtained from our senses.

Episteme According to Foucault, the episteme of a particular historical period consists of the rules and conventions which govern the establishment of new knowledge at the time.

Epistemology The branch of philosophy which examines the grounds upon which we believe something to be true.

Existentialism A philosophy often associated with Jean-Paul Sartre which emphasizes the freedom of human beings to determine their own way in life.

Modern The period from the early nineteenth century onwards which was typified by the rise of technology, and the application of science to society.

Positivism The assertion that methods of the physical sciences, such as experiments and hypothesis testing, are the most appropriate ones for investigating society.

Postmodern This period has been characterized by the advent of computers and electronic communication. In many areas it has seen a decline in manufacturing industry, and the development of a knowledge-based society.

Structuralism The assertion that the structures of society such as the institutions of business, law, education and industry exert more influence on individuals than people are able to exert on institutions.

Taking it further

Works by Michel Foucault in English translation

Foucault, M. (1971) *Madness and Civilization: A history of insanity in the age of reason*. London: Tavistock.

Foucault, M. (1972) *The Archaeology of Knowledge*. New York: Harper and Row.

Foucault, M. (1974) *The Order of Things: An archaeology of the human sciences*. London: Tavistock.

Foucault, M. (1975) *The Birth of the Clinic: An archaeology of medical perception*. New York: Vintage.

Foucault, M. (1976) *Mental Illness and Psychology*. London: Harper and Row.

Foucault, M. (1977) *Discipline and Punish: The birth of the prison*. London: Penguin.

Foucault, M. (1979) *The History of Sexuality, Vol. 1: An introduction*. London: Penguin.

Works concerned with Foucault

Boyne, R. (1990) *Foucault and Derrida: The other side of reason*. London: Unwin Hyman.

Davidson, A., ed. (1997) *Foucault and His Interlocutors*. Chicago: University of Chicago Press.

Dreyfus, H. and Rabinow, P. (1982) *Michel Foucault: Beyond structuralism and hermeneutics*. Chicago: Chicago University Press.

Faubion, J.D., ed. (2002) *Michel Foucault: Power*. London: Penguin.

Gordon, C., ed. (1980) *Michel Foucault: Power/Knowledge – selected interviews and other writings, 1972–1977*. Hemel Hempstead, Herts: Harvester Wheatsheaf.

Gutting, G. (1989) *Michel Foucault's Archaeology of Scientific Reason*. Cambridge: Cambridge University Press.

Hoy, D., ed. (1986) *Foucault: A critical reader*. Oxford: Blackwell.

Kelly, M.G.E. (2008) *The Political Philosophy of Michel Foucault*. New York: Routledge.

Kritzman, L.D., ed. (1990) *Michel Foucault: Politics, philosophy, culture – interviews and other writings, 1977–1984*. New York: Routledge.

Lemert, C.C. and Gillan, G. (1982) *Michel Foucault: Social theory and transgression*. New York: Columbia University Press.

Levy, N. (2001) *Being Up-to-Date: Foucault, Sartre and postmodernity*. New York: Peter Lang.

Merquior, J.G. (1991) *Foucault*, 2nd edn. London: Fontana.

Miller, J. (1993) *The Passion of Michel Foucault*. New York: Simon and Schuster.

O'Farrell, C. (1989) *Foucault: Historian or philosopher?* London: Macmillan.

Palmer, D.D. (1998) *Structuralism and Poststructuralism*. New York: Writers and Readers.

Peterson, A. and Bunton, R. (1997) *Foucault, Health and Medicine*. London: Routledge.

Poster, M. (1984) *Foucault, Marxism and History*. Cambridge: Polity.

Rabinow, P., ed. (1984) *The Foucault Reader*. Pantheon: New York.

Rabinow, P., ed. (2000) *Michel Foucault: Ethics – subjectivity and truth*. London: Penguin.

Rajchman, J. (1985) *Michel Foucault and the Freedom of Philosophy*. New York: Columbia University Press.

Sheridan, A. (1980) *Michel Foucault: The will to truth*. London: Tavistock.

Shumway, D.R. (1992) *Michel Foucault*. Charlottesville: University Press of Virginia.

Smart, B. (1983) *Foucault, Marxism and Critique*. London: Routledge and Kegan Paul.

Index

Credits